DANCING THROUGH
THE MAZE

William Leonardi

DANCING THROUGH THE MAZE

Gilmour House
Warwick, New York

Published by Gilmour House
A Division of R & R Writers/Agents
4 Sly Street
Warwick, NY 10990-3572

phone: 845.986.1694
fax: 845.986.4290
E-mail: gilmourhouse@aol.com

Copyright © 2008 by William Leonardi
ISBN: 0965375366
Library of Congress Control Number: 2008928112

First Edition

164 pages, $22.00

Printed in the United States of America

Design by Paul Vartanian, Print Solutions

For gemstones that sparkle even in darkness:
My wife Lucinda
My daughter Lee

ACKNOWLEDGEMENTS

A very special thank you to my publisher and editor: Ms. Rae Lindsay. She came into my maze and became my "Dream Catcher."

And thank you to Guy Burton, leader of the Warwick Valley Writers' Association, and its members: Marge Adamo, Joan Corser-Gay, Lynne Digby, Sonia Lynch, Anne Thornton, and Marge Von See.

In memory of a fallen angel, Tom Sardo

Author's note:

The story is true. Some of the events—the timing and place have been altered slightly, to protect those who have fallen.

Many thanks to Lieutenant Colonel Donald E.(Mofak)Cathcart, United States Marine Corps Retired, for the use of pictures from his web site: Mofak.com. He came through for me at a critical time... and became a new friend. Thank you for your wonderful help.

Magic theater. Entrance not for everyone. For madmen only!
STEPPENWOLF
Hermann Hesse, Berlin, 1927

PREFACE

No one told me there was a "raptor" living inside me, irritating every cell of my body so that one day I would leap free from the Earth, and fly away. Not one person told me that, only the "maze." Its convoluted passages echoing secret messages, wafting gentle breezes that whispered against my ears. The maze! My life's invisible blueprint allowing me infinite choices, letting me stumble, even retreat at times back through the unknown, but not to the beginning. That door had closed long before. Shut tight when my mother and father nodded to creation. And it made no difference if I crawled, or walked, or ran in a frenzy toward the future; there was just one pathway out. Every corridor, every blind alley, every wrong turn, and every right one brought me closer and closer to aviation. *Should I believe this? Do I believe?* It is an argument for logic and wise men whose wisdom filters into the future . . . though, without conclusion.

My initiation into the cockpit was not easy. There were many obstacles, anxieties, even close calls with death. Was it the maze that protected me? Were angels watching over me? *Will I ever know?* Quien Sabe?

INTRODUCTION

Birth is not necessarily freedom for mankind, not his intellect, reason, nor his dreams. Even after the cuts and the snips and the cries, there *can* remain a tether. And there are no instruments powerful enough to sever life from it. So youth moves from one protective labyrinth to another, learning adjustments to his or her environment under protective feminine eyes. Cat eyes. Acute, sensitive, and at times, wicked. Sometimes they watch with iridescence, glowering and measuring each move, every second. In daylight they can cast out invisible tacky threads—limitations laced with agenda, allowing exploration to progress only so far. There is unspoken power in such suspicious eyes. Female eyes. Eyes of motherhood. Eyes full of expectation between two, mother and child, but satisfaction for only one.

They trapped me early on, shading my impatience so desperate to reach high into a dream. Imagination and flight throbbed deep in my soul. In time, I realized the feline stares were not ratcheting back on me, but rather on the cat.

She was unaware of the sad price unchecked nurturing claimed. To her, protection was self-fulfilling gratification, though she never realized the viscosity of protectionism. There were no seas offering to transit me smoothly into maturity. Yet, my life was entwined in the maze.

One day I knew freedom would come. It had to. And the beginning of the end would be swift for the cat, her dominance

3

summarily destroyed by the unleashed *Alpha*. It was always there in my weave—the Alpha—finally unlocked one day with ferocity. That cataclysmic bolt for independence, identity, life and freedom. Each in its own way a natural elixir, mighty enough to sever "nurturism." Man is wrapped in it. Strength is his simplicity of existence. His genetic pre-disposition to roam free, just as beauty, security and nurture are fundamental to women.

I was born to run free. Had I been born African, Masai, tests of "my coming of age" would have happened sooner. I didn't realize this at first. Nothing appeared etched in concrete pillars to discover, or buried deep in the black tar of Brooklyn streets. Certainly not a world apart on the Mara—the plains of Africa, where the rite of passage is judged with a spear and measured in the death of a lion.

For me, that rite, that growth in self-esteem and confidence came on the wing and in the skies. It floated above me, waiting to be conquered. So I set off for the adventure.

I was like the Masai. Older, true, but not entirely different. We both hunted courage. Me in a third dimension. My coming of age waited above me. All I needed were wings. They came unexpectedly later in life, yet they were there all along in the maze, my convoluted path to flight. So I learned to fly. To understand the thread that weaves into "self" and glorifies the soul, and which inspires confidence, humbles compassion and dignifies respect to love. That inner sanctuary where flesh fuses with spirit and life is offered back to creation on cupped hands of dignity. The raptor taught me to stand tall.

I raced high above the Earth—my Mora, floating, diving, climbing, pushing the speed of my plane to its limits. I attacked and destroyed. It was exhilarating, and at times frightening, clashing into the unknown like the young Masai boy. Me, armed with a demon machine, while he had just a simple spear.

Aviation freed me to look carefully at myself. To believe in myself. Something all raptors are born to and accept with grace, but I had to learn the process. I transformed gently, subtly, the way innocence gives way to maturity. Then flew away from our planet's constraints.

I bullied my way through ice and snow. Tangled with belligerent angry clouds. I punched through rain, shrugged off lightning, skidded down to Earth through howling winds. It was surgery on every one of them. I accomplished it on a wing and a prayer. For Orville and Wilbur Wright . . . I owe them more than a simple thank you. I owe them life. Mine.

Dancing Through The Maze

AN END BEFORE THE START

I never saw it. But I felt it. A steel rod ripping into my left eye. Searing, agonizing, knee-buckling pain shooting through my head, dropping me where I stood. My horrific screams bringing my brother running.

We were both bored, looking for something to do that summer's day back in 1955. Most of our friends were away on vacation. It was just the two of us, sitting around idle under a blazing yellow sun, both of us drenched by stifling humidity.

"Want to play war?" I asked. My brother looked at me as though I was some form of lower life, a bothersome pest. I suppose when you are older, you see things from a different perspective. After all, he'd been walking this planet almost two years longer than I.

"No, but I'll play cops and robbers," he answered back.

"Why don't we just choose?" I argued. "Odds we play war. Evens, it's cops." He looked at me unhappily for a second. High school mathematics helped me understand his expression. *The whole is equal to the sum of the parts.* A ninety percent scowl meandered across his perspiring face, meaning, "I'm not happy, twerp." But there was also a ten percent gleam glistening from his brown eyes. Extrapolating, I took that to mean, okay.

We both stood up facing one another. "On three," he said.

"One! Two! Three!" We both shot out our fingers. I threw one, he threw two.

"Hey, odd wins!" I said triumphantly. "It's war. We can play out back, and shoot missiles through that hole in the garage wall. A perfect launch pad for rockets," I said. "Anyway, It'll be a lot cooler there." He thought about this for a moment. I watched him closely, his head turning this way, then that, deep in thought. I waited impatiently, looking up and down our deserted street.

"Come on. Let's go!" I said, in frustration.

He was reluctant, but we both jumped from the steps, making our way through the basement and out toward the garage.

Most of the homes in our neighborhood were attached to one another. They were nondescript architectural achievements, two story square boxes planted on cinder block foundations. You either parked your car out front on the street, or had to drive around the corner to an alleyway, leading to the back of the house.

Unfortunately, there was no direct entrance from the garage into the house. After parking your car, you had to walk out, close the overhead doors, then turn and walk down a side walkway. It was another twenty feet to a door that opened into the basement. Some architect's clever attempt at magic, but his sleight of hand poorly executed. Why here? It's in the wrong place.

Towering cinder block walls rose up on each side of this pathway. To me, It was like looking up from the floor of the Grand Canyon.

Masons must have understood the problems of close-quarter living. They etched a deep groove in the concrete path, mid-way between my house and our neighbor's. An undeclared zone of neutrality, or combat—depending upon a family's social congeniality. If you didn't like the people next door, come winter, you'd shovel away snow, but only up to that line, no more. In summer, you swept the concrete clean, but your side only. So, a nasty, unspoken feud tended to perpetuate itself.

Fire escapes linked my home with the next. If you leaned out real far from the kitchen window, and your neighbor did likewise, you could almost shake hands or exchange necessities, like milk or sugar, or whatever. But only if you liked them. The middle of the fire escape was neutral, like that etched line in the pathway far below us. Some people put out small potted trees or plants as a buffer. You knew things were not going well between them, then. But that's how close we lived. A different world up here on the second floor. Three stories up, if you counted the basement.

Sometimes I would have to climb that Eiffel Tower of rusting wrought iron, when I forgot my keys. We always left our kitchen window unlocked. I was pretty agile back then, fleet of foot and stealthy. I never unhitched the safety ladders, too much trouble to re-secure them. Sometimes I'd catch my downstairs neighbor in her underwear, as I wrestled my way up. It would surprise both of us. She'd stop, facing me in shock, crossing her arms over her breasts. I'd stop too, wild-eyed, gawking, hanging by one arm like a fool, from one of the railings. She seemed to enjoy my sudden intrusion and predicament, and after a few seconds, did a sensual pirouette, giving this young boy an inkling of what was yet to come? I loved her sheer kitchen curtains, but even more, that she always kept them parted. I nearly lost my grip, awe-struck. Wow! After that, I remembered to forget my keys a lot.

Because of our location, the back alley received little direct sunlight, so it was much cooler there, but also more boring. No place to sit, no people to watch, no music filtering through the air. Still, not a bad place for us to improvise war.

Someone had drilled a quarter-sized hole through the width of one of the cinder blocks, in the foundation wall. Why, I have no idea. There was enough light to see through it, that is, into the garage if you peeked from the outside; or, from the inside, you could see out to our neighbor's garage. My brother stood inside, while I manned the outside.

It was amazing, watching a twelve-inch piece of steel welding rod burst from the cinder block like a rocket. When my brother struck, it shot out in a wicked arc—piercing airspace above the neutral zone—pinging like a ricocheting bullet into my neighbor's wall. There were dozens of small chips gouged from the blocks by these forceful impacts.

I stood close to the wall. When it was my turn to hit, I placed the rod in the hole, leaving the tip exposed, then smacked it with all my might. The rod shot through the wall, passing my brother, streaking across the interior of the garage into the opposite wall. Anything can fly if it has enough speed. Wings are not really necessary. We had established a simple launch signal. He'd shout from inside, "Are you ready!" and I'd yell back from the outside "Clear!" Then he'd whack it with a two-by-four. We reversed the calls when it was my turn. Each time though, we struck harder, trying to send the rod farther and faster.

One of my shots really took off, and it was up to my brother to match that distance, or make it *ping* even louder. He placed the rod in the hole. I had my face pressed against the outside cinder blocks, squinting so I could watch him load the tube. I didn't hear him yell "Ready?" He hit, just before I could shout "Clear!" There was no time to duck, but I did flinch slightly. My head and body snapped backwards from the impact, dropping me instantly to the ground.

I was blinded by white hot pain, rolling back and forth on the ground, screaming. Blood oozed from my eye and with it—my sight.

Neighbors heard my cries and rushed to help.

I remember waking up in the hospital. I think my parents and brother were there at my side.

Doctors did what they could, clearing away metal filings, flushing out debris, then setting bandages. They told me I was lucky. The rod had ripped through the cornea, tearing a small piece of the iris, but not the lens. And more fortunate, the vitreous sac behind the pupil had not ruptured. But the rod did puncture just below my eyebrow, chipping some bone from the bridge of my nose. Would I regain my sight? "Only time would tell," they said.

There was a message inscribed on that rod for me. A warning ricocheting down crooked passages in the maze: Those dreams you've had, young man? Last night? Last week? Last year? Of flight, of freedom and adventure like Gann and St. Exupery? Savor what remains of them. Because ?. . .

It was difficult for my mother, bathing my eye every few hours with warm water. This went on for well over a month. There wasn't much she could do for the pain. It came in waves. The same hurt anyone would experience if a particle of dirt was suddenly blown into your eye. That debilitating pain as you frantically circle your eyelid, hoping to dislodge whatever it is pressing down, trying to scribe a channel in the tissue. The harder you move it, the worse it gets. I had a scab in mine driving me insane. Magnify the hurt ten-fold, that's how it felt. I was restrained at times so I couldn't touch the wound and do more damage. School was on hold, and it seemed, so was my life. Healing took a long time, a few months in fact. I wore a dark eye patch shielding half of life from myself. Eventually, after many more months, my vision returned. But would it be accurate again, good enough for me to fly? Only the maze held that answer.

Dancing Through The Maze

BEGINNINGS

Brooklyn, New York. That extreme western city of Long Island, where the guns of Fort Hamilton, long ago, protected the Lower Narrows River from the sweep of "them" off the Atlantic. *Oh, them!* Those foreigners from: Italy, England, Ireland, Germany, and Scandinavia. The years 1892, until 1954, were a godsend for, *them*. All twelve million of *them*.

They swept inland off the Atlantic, around Bay Ridge, Brooklyn—my home on Long Island—a rifle shot distance separating me, and every one of *them,* from the rest of the United States. They chugged up the Hudson River with tear-filled eyes, passing the Statue of Liberty, only to make landfall on another island—Ellis Island. One of America's welcome wagons filled with disdain. When cleared by customs, they were guided away with a pat on the back for a good life, then directed across steel bridges back to Long Island and Brooklyn. That crowded borough of New York City, where black streets form ice skating rinks in a deep winter freeze, and asphalt turns soft in a summer's volcanic heat. A place where trees are a miracle and grass a relief. Where wealth and language change block-to-block. Where our home sits just inland from the Narrows, secured tightly between high-rise apartments bristling like grown crystals. And above me, in a narrow ribbon of sky, an endless stream of airliners approaching La Guardia airport. Powerful machines spewing black and white vapor trails that seared endless lines of longed-for-freedom into my brain. "Magic carpets" riding velvet dreams for a trapped young mind. *Someday! One day!* I would soar free . . . and join them. *But how?*

The New World Napolitanos looked on with contempt at arriving Sicilianos. How an "island" Italian young man bullied his way past my mother's "mainland" heritage, I'll never know. But, somehow he managed it, marrying against bigotry. *Love is blind, isn't it?* So, I grew up tasting bitter feelings ever present between the two families. Different strains of blood thudding with all the tension and histrionics of Italian prejudice coursing my veins. It is the first born male in most Italian families who is lavished upon. As number two I had to live in shadows gathered and sheltered beneath the wings of a matriarch. Not because it was my mother's choice. All avenues of happiness for her had crumbled years before my birth. I was her escape. Her rescue from a troubled marriage. Everyone in the "family" and even our tight community knew that good Italian women don't divorce. Her options beyond motherhood were limited. If she could have, my mother would have exchanged death in paradise for happiness on Earth. She pounded on Heaven's door in desperation. In her mind there was always that distant belief; that divine intervention would reward her and ease her pain. She knelt for Novenas on swollen knees and prayed. She bowed her head, covered with lace, firing pleas to God. She crushed ivory Rosary Beads till they bled, praying like a saint. She recited the Lord's Prayer with every ounce of energy left in her soul. She struck at her breast invoking Mary, "Hailing" her the required ten times. And she ended in tears as she always did with, "Glory Be To The Father," waiting for salvation to explode before her eyes. Day after day this was her routine. She prayed furiously past the wings of Seraphim anxious for a short cut to the Lord. It was useless, though. Nothing came, nor would it ever. She cursed under her breath and held me tight to her chest for joy, even as I struggled, pulling back. My leash never far from her side as I began to stray. Her aloneness almost too much for her to bear or for me to watch.

On those rare occasions when I asked my father for advice, his succinct reply would be, "If you want something, go get it!" That was that. We never had much of a relationship. When I spoke to my mother for advice, I'd hear: "Are you sure? That's dangerous isn't it? Be careful. Wouldn't you rather do ?. . ."

I grew through puberty with dichotomy raging in me: Freedom versus entrapment. Aggression warring against caution. Imagination fighting involution. Where any of this could possibly play out, I had no idea. But my life was unraveling in turmoil. In the back of my mind, lingering anxiety over the sight in my left eye. I still longed to fly.

But great things were forecast for me. I was to be the all important rising star. The Sicilian hope and dream to boost our family status. Not even a teenager, and my life had already narrowed by Marcus Welby dreams—physician extraordinaire—for my mother, not me. I was adolescent walking death, because I hadn't learned to live for myself. Escape into freedom is the essence of all animals. I was one myself, fighting family and educational pressures dragging on me like chains. I snarled and tore at the restraints.

School was prison. There was no excitement resonating off those beige walls. The only subjects of any interest, and the only ones of freshness were in the sciences. How I turned toward them I don't know. I've wondered that, time and again. If there was an answer it came in sudden glimmers, like witnessing the wonder of a mirage for the first time. That vague undulating apparition so real, yet so mysterious and intriguing.

Science offered clarity to puzzlement and I began to see and understand the "how and why" of life on our fragile planet. Our lone oasis drifting against the stars. I needed answers. Something I found difficult discerning from the study of language, or history, or economics. Scientists on the other hand were realists. Archeological detectives prying into the unknown. They smiled at ridicule, turning away from its naiveté. "No," was never a consideration for them. They were driven by intense passion and wild imagination. Each new discovery they labored to uncover overwrote previously held

Gymnastics instilled confidence in me. I helped instruct others as a gym Leader. I'm on the bottom row, third from the right. After too long a pause I made it into college, Southern Illinois University. Upon graduation, I was drafted for the Vietnam Conflict. In 1968, I joined the Navy, rather than be inducted into the Army, and began flight training.

reasoning. Some of it, because of its impenetrable logic, became physical law. And over time, these theorems were absorbed worldwide, easing societies forward, though under tighter constraints.

These adventurers became my friends. My heroes. Artisans in their own right, living far outside the group. Maybe I was isolated from society like them? Maybe I am a loner just like them?

There had to be a different life beyond the breadth of my shoulders. Somewhere far from the imposed blinders of tenements and office buildings. I was suffocating, yet found intrigue and hope in that thin sliver of sky above me. There was no containment there, just release and escape. My mind leaped to the deep vibrato of each passing airplane, their spewing white contrails flowing like lines of freedom. Messages magically written across the heavens showing a way, offering me hope as no one had done before, or ever would. *Can't you see this, Mother, Dad? I was meant to grace the clouds. To link with the stars.*

Books only reinforced my wandering spirit. Those exhilarating sagas of men and women living life on the edge, unafraid, fighting for their beliefs when necessary. Aviation would become my salvation. Only I had to get there, first. I think it was there all along in the maze. I know that it was!

I needed a mentor, but there wasn't anyone to point the way. School dragged on, and I drifted above a sea of students like a dark cloud. And yet, there was gradual change in my thoughts as the urgency for independence grew in importance. Its evolution was imperceptible to my family and my teachers. But it billowed nonetheless. Powerful and unstoppable.

It came from my love of reading and it came through in sports. In gymnastics I found strength and courage to trust myself. In literature, words were a secret fuel illuminating my imagination.

There was excitement and power concealed beneath the covers of books. Exquisite flavors of light cultivating the tongue and palate of my mind. Buried treasures waiting patiently to be discovered, particularly in biographies. So it was easy to leave the moment and forget myself, dissolving deep in pages where time loses all meaning.

For an eternity I slipped into the muscle and bone of great fighters like Graziano and Robinson and Marciano. I was electrifying thought, piercing wonders of the universe like Einstein and Sagan and Hawkins. I strapped into the cockpit, racing silver wings like Gann and Earhart and St. Exupery. Their exploits whisking me into that inexplicable dimension beyond time itself. Each of these men and women instrumental in my escape from a *sane society.* And every one of them in their own way, a gemstone adorning the richness in my life.

In the gymnasium I flew in graceful arcs around the high bar. I moved to a ballet twisting and rolling up and down the wooden arms of parallel bars. I jumped in eloquent precision and timed sequence across handles of the pummel horse. I was pure strength conquering the heights of the rope climb. Physical evasion from the confines of concrete walls.

But graduation was more a relief than an accomplishment. Classmates remained anonymous. I don't even remember their faces. My friends did not walk in that crowd. High school was simply the government's bureaucratic satisfaction for another of its citizens. I was allowed to dress in a black cap and gown, then ushered away.

And written in invisible ink on my diploma were caveats: You are old enough now to be on your own. Vote if you like in elections. You are authorized to pull the trigger, yank the pin, drop bombs and kill other human beings in war. Be free to drown your sins in alcohol—you're allowed. You are alone with yourself to vanish into obscurity in the work force.

For two more years I had to endure the agony of a meaningless job. I worked deep below ground in New York City, riding a subway between Brooklyn and Manhattan in utter darkness. I labored in the bowels of a skyscraper, hefting crates in a black cavern. My home-

Brooklyn was just as dark and empty when I returned. Someone in jest had yanked the plug on the sun. None of my screams could restore it. There had to be something better for me. But where? I needed help and I needed guidance.

It came out of nowhere from a friend. An immigrant educator. A professor of linguistics who had left Germany for a better life in the United States—just like my grandparents. He had tasted war and its evil, turning against his homeland and his roots, and moved West.

Doctor Helmut Hartwick lived briefly at our home, and I'm certain he saw the despair written on my face. It was only through his efforts and persistence that I gained entrance to Southern Illinois University, the same college where he was to be a department chairman. I jumped at the opportunity and ambushed it.

Every moment, every book, every lecture, every laboratory, I devoured. It was obsession on my part. A four year journey and ascent up a towering path of knowledge. I made it, though. I climbed free of an abyss, pale and thin, but made it. And in the end, a scholarship to graduate school came, as well as acceptance into medical school. Yet, the maze held a different direction for me. It came with the draft. And it came with war—Vietnam. The most defining moment in my life.

Uncle Sam needed me and said, "Come with me, my son," ushering me deeper into the maze. For a while it was peaceful there, neither one of us speaking at first, until I said, "I'll go, Sir. But under conditions."

"Oh? And what might they be?" he replied, somewhat startled, but a gleam shimmering like magic from his piercing dark eyes.

"I want to fly. Fly in the Navy."

". . . Well . . ." he paused for a few seconds deep in thought, then said. "I'll tell you. See that junction a little further down? Where this path joins a 'T.' If I were *you*, I'd make a right when you get there," then he pushed me away. I started forward but stopped briefly, turning to look at him. But he was already gone.

19

I moved on, turning right as he suggested at the junction, a few minutes later I found myself at an exit. In fact, it was an entrance into another maze. It was bright there; that I remember. Clouds above me breaking apart as I walked along, and a blazing yellow sun streaming down, inviting me to a new home: Pensacola, Florida, headquarters for Naval Aviation Schools Command. I had passed the Navy pilot test and was being offered a commission as a Naval Aviator. My chase toward an elusive rainbow cradling a childhood dream was closing. In the distance I saw glitter sparkling off gold wings. It was within my grasp, even with that childhood scar in my eye. But, now I faced a triumvirate decision, *which pathway do I take?*

Should I resign my scholarship as a teaching assistant to the physiology department, at Southern? Should I walk away from everything I had studied so long and hard to achieve—a medical school education at Bologna University? Should I say, " yes," to Naval flight training, even though it means going to war?

Graduate school was safe. So was Bologna. But flying was an answer to a dream. A future I needed to live in. The mystery of raptors still searching for me. And joining the Navy was an alternative to the agony of the draft.

What will it be, William? Safety . . . and future sorrow? Or, excitement and freedom? Uncle Sam wants your answer, now!

My decision was not that difficult—there *was* no choice, life had already seen to that. I was at a pre-set moment in my own history—in the maze, standing alone, looking down three intriguing corridors.

I could easily turn down the assistantship. Italy, on the other hand, satisfied a mother's hope and long-held aspiration for a son. She never felt or understood the conflict stirring within me. That damn need to be free, pulsing through my brain, pounding deep in my veins. Naval aviation was poised to hand me something so very special, something my mother could not. A dream. I knew there might never come a second chance.

20

In the end, after much thought, I tore away guilt. Broke a heart. But saved a life. My own. I would fly.

So, I packed up my things and left Illinois for Brooklyn.

Dancing Through The Maze

DREAM CATCHER

June 20th, 1967. Freedom! The day a rainbow burst from my eyes. Oh, yes! Today. When I finally waved a flag of triumph symbolically—looking out at the world from high on a summit. I found that magic exit in the maze and looked beyond to an entryway with diamond eyes. Aviation sparkled, throbbing just one heartbeat away over that threshold. I stepped in.

That was six years after a young teenager's hope for the future was scrawled in wet ink, gliding across the gloss pages of a high school yearbook. Twenty-one years wondering the meaning of a recurring dream. A brash answer to an impersonal query: What will the future bring to you? It was me, William Peter, that young man who penned without hesitation and succinctly: Aviation. Nothing more, nothing less. So, the journey began. I never realized how long it might be. It was compelling, and the passion became fuel for my mind, driving me into uncharted regions. It could be elusive, though. Chasing itself season-after-season without purpose, because no one was there pointing the way. Not even the ghost of my living father.

Yet, there were some who saw through my chaos, believing in me. Not all, just a special few. The Lakota and the Sioux were a few who understood. They had their "Dream Catcher." No one knows how or why they found me. Maybe it was I who found them. Yet, they offered the "Catcher" to me, with humility. Its web glittering, and the elegant weave of its filaments splayed apart, ready to capture.

Dancing Through The Maze

For a few precious moments I witnessed its magic, the gift of a dream brought to me. It was all part of the maze, how my life intersected with theirs.

But I had to return this revered Catcher to its rightful owners, with all the respect it deserved and with love. It, too, required freedom. To be passed on to others for their chance in this world. It raised a hope from transparency to reality and allowed me to treasure each day. It was never meant as a possession. Neither is my soul. Yet, it is something we all have in our humanism. The essence of humanity. This wonderful mind. I looked in awe at the Catcher one last time, and thanked him again for my dream.. . . *I woke into a turquoise sky, finding home in pale clouds, and life in fresh winds.*

Six long years, and the ink had finally dried in that high school year book. It was time to close the cover, forever. I never did break the circle, not at the beginning or at the end. It wasn't necessary. I'm just living within its mystery.

Flight school was not to be an easy journey. It had its loves and it had its sorrows.

BABY STEPS

The Navy and I were symbionts. No, *vampires*! Each of us sucking blood from the other because of selfish needs. They sliced and probed and demanded until my body ran on empty. And *I*, in my anger, clawed and devoured and absorbed their secrets until their history grew into my flesh.

The Naval recruiters had excavated me from the depths of dirty city streets, whisking me off to one of their factories to be processed like a rare metal. After twelve weeks of molding and stamping I was shot from an exit, groomed and ready to lead men to their deaths.

That was not the end, though. The Navy needed more. To sculpt me into a duplicate of the fearsome "Red Baron," into a life of survival in that third dimension. But I had never even seen a cockpit or sat in one, so this grandiose idea seemed ridiculous.

Nonetheless, with very little flight time, this middleclass Brooklyn boy was taught to fight—*to dogfight*—and rid an enemy from his tail. I was forced to become a boxer, a slugger, a contender; to think, then punish my plane to the point of insanity because what appeared in front of my eyes was no less dangerous than what was closing in on my back. I entered a brotherhood, learning the choreography of the battle—of engagement and disengagement—maneuvers like the: "Immelmann," the "Half Cuban Eight," the "Split S," the "Loop." Each aggressive twist and snap intended to shake a killer from my "six-o-clock" position, then bring my own guns to bear on target. To unleash *h-e-l-l* on him, and zipper a torrent of lead into his machine; watching with elation as his engine explodes and his wings disintegrate, and he plummets out-of-control, to earth. *Ohhh. . .the sensual pleasure of war!*

And thanks to my own government's philosophy, and the enemy's politics, the situation was reduced down in simplicity to: Kill, or be killed. *It's him, or me!*

Yet, all of this was a choice. Mine. And mine alone.

1969: my official Navy picture after my first solo flight in the T-34.

It's official: "alone and unassisted," I completed my first solo flight.

INITIATIONS

Where were the angels for Robert Wesley when his plane left the carrier deck just seconds behind me? Where were they when his engine exploded in a fireball, and his speed and altitude ceased to be companions, and his plane plunged through a safe cushion of air into angry green sea? Where were they then?

I saw him die in a hopeless roll to the left, striking the water in flames, pieces of the fuselage and geysers of water spraying high into the air. And then the huge warship barreling down—unable to turn, crushing what remained of the wreckage into the churning sea. He was gone in an instant, twenty-seven years of life vanished . . . gone . . . erased, as though he had never existed.

Robert died one Friday morning as the nation's cities awoke and crowds gathered and horns blared. He died as children sighed awake and bade goodbye to their families, and schools threw open their doors. He died as the ill and anguished prayed for more time and promised their souls, and all anyone could do was offer them hope.

My friend Robert died alone, though. Not as a lover. Not as a husband. And not as a father. He was denied forever the joy of love's mystery and its miraculous power of creation. Six months earlier, we were immortal flight cadets defying the gods, daring them with our controlled arrogance.

I watched him crash as my own plane climbed effortlessly to altitude, banking with ease as I made a left turn, reversing my course back toward the ship. For a moment I didn't hear the hellacious staccato of the engine or feel the chill from the tornadic winds whipping through the cockpit. Yet I was freezing, my thin flight suit offering little comfort and my mind numbed by the accident.

Things were happening too fast now. I saw the rescue helicopter as a gray blur hovering above the crash site, its rotor wash laying down streaks of white spray. It passed beneath the wing of my plane and I caught a glimpse of divers already in the water, but I knew it was too late. Any second now, I was certain the Captain of the Wasp would halt our qualifications, ordering us overhead to rendezvous for the flight back to Pensacola.

But that call never came. Suddenly, I was abeam the stern of the carrier, flying way too fast and too high. I was next in the pattern and struggled to block the accident from my mind, to forget Robert, and get myself down. I scrambled through the landing checklist, shoving the propeller control into full low-pitch for drag. The sudden change in rpm nearly over-sped the engine, and the plane lurched in protest. "Slow down," I chastised myself, then continued reading and touching each item on the list. By now the ship was less than a mile in front of me.

"Gear? Down!"

"Flaps? Full down!"

"Speed brake? Damn!" I nearly forgot the speed brake, and quickly thumbed the switch on the throttle, feeling the plane pitch-up in response as the slotted panel shot open into the slip stream.

"Speed brake," I repeated again. "Down!"

"Tailhook? Down!" The canopy was already open. There was hardly time to think as I rolled into the slot at 250 feet and 100 miles per hour. The mirror landing system lights slid into view. "Five-Four has the ball, 1000 pounds," I spoke into the microphone, my mouth dry, sounding high-pitched and hollow, betraying my fear. The reply from the Landing Signal Officer (LSO) was curt, "Roger Ball," but did not acknowledge my fuel status.

Down I came, focusing and reciting the 'litany of life' they had drummed into us during carrier landing practice at Barin Airfield,

Pensacola. *Center the ball (meatball) in the green horizontal lights. Power equals airplane attitude. Never, ever, lose control of your airspeed!* The advice became an admonishment, and a cadence: *Meatball, power, airspeed. Meatball, power, airspeed.* It buzzed over and over again in my brain as I looked repeatedly from the mirror landing system back to my flight instruments. The closer I got to the carrier, the faster I scanned the deck and my gauges. The LSO was talking and I suppose I made the proper corrections, yet I don't remember doing it. I held the "ball" dead on—in between the green-lighted horizontal bar. It was the precise vertical path to the ship, and as long as I did not allow it to go low and turn red, I'd make it to the deck and not strike the fantail.

Fifty feet from the stern the green lights flashed. I chopped the power immediately, waiting for the gear to slam onto the wood deck. When they hit, I instantly jammed in full power in case the tailhook skipped the wires and I found myself careening back down the deck. But I was snagged—thrown forcefully into my shoulder harness, as if the wheels had ploughed into a trough of thick mud.

It happened so fast, when the force of the deceleration eased and my eyes opened in recoil, I found I had touched down in the land of Oz. A featureless, monochromatic drab gray "Emerald City." A land without color, without flowers and trees. An island without music or gaiety or laughter. Little bug-eyed people rushed my plane like a death squad. I felt I was under attack.

In a sense I was. They spoke a menacing language with their bodies, charging toward me, frantically waving their hands, flailing their arms, kicking the air with their legs. But their language was not open to interpretation. They stood next to me, fearless. "Move forward!" they commanded.

"Turn right!"

"Turn left!"

"Tailhook up!"

"Flaps set!"

"Check fuel!"

"Controls—deflect!"

I punished my plane with as much aggression as they threw at me. They were guiding me on a road toward freedom—through narrow confines, in a direction where the almighty Oz presides.

I saw him out of the corner of my eye. He was taller than the others and more majestic, with a slender build, but bug-eyed too, like his subjects, dark goggles distorting his face. His movements were imperiously slow, not the least bit contrived, yet regal and commanding. This was the Launch Officer—the wise and powerful "Oz." He stood like a God, and at this very moment he was my salvation, my escape home.

I crept toward him, cautiously. And like an unflinching statue, he scrutinized my every move. When I was at the proper distance from him, he slowly raised his left arm above his head, balled a tight fist, and snapped it sharply in the air. "STOP!" I jammed my feet on the brakes in fear, and four-tons of killing machine genuflected to a stop next to him. He stared at me so intently that my eyes began to water—daring me to budge so much as an inch—without his permission. I froze in place. He glared and I swam in my own sweat. Then, after what seemed an eternity, as my legs throbbed in pain holding the brakes, the Wizard raised his right hand to his shoulder. His index finger snapped out beyond the others, like a switchblade. Slowly he began making circles in the air.

"Throttle up!" I did as he said, and the engine went from angry to furious. The rhythmic explosions from the exhaust were deafening. The propeller ripped the moist air into white vapor. Faster and faster his hand twirled, until I had the throttle pinned against the firewall. The plane danced and jumped beneath me. The instrument panel shook so violently on its rubber mounts, I could hardly read the gauges. And my legs gave up with a mind of their own, pulsing and twitching, trying to hold back 1,425 pissed-off horses.

The Wizard seemed to be enjoying my agony. "Hold your brakes! Increase your rpm!" When I thought I couldn't hold it a second longer, his fingers mashed the air even more violently. He was waiting for my salute. Only then would he transfer power to me, and give me my freedom. The instruments seemed liquefied, but the needles inside pointed reasonably well, so I snapped my right hand to my helmet. I thought I saw a smile spread across his lips. Then in one graceful lunge, like a swordsmen about to deliver a fatal blow, he shifted his weight far over his bent right knee and touched the deck.

"Launch! You are free!"

I waited a second longer before committing myself down the flight deck. In that hesitation an eerie feeling swept over me, as though I was suddenly shot back in time . . . then returned. It was illusionary, but nonetheless—real. The sort of feeling you experience trying to make sense of a sun-drenched mirage. My brain, confused by the wavering reality of it, ignoring logic and science and the cries of fraud. In the blink of an eye, a contraction of my heart, the surge of blood to my brain, I speared a moment in history . . . tugging it back to the present. An exact overlay of a scene from a past life. A life I don't remember, yet saw for a split second through the eyes of a pilot readying himself for combat—about thirty years ago. It was war in the Pacific then. World War Two, a similar carrier I was about to depart. She battled in the Philippine Sea, at Tarawa and Luzon. She was pummeled in the Marianas, and at Leyte Gulf, and Wake Island. I was not a hero in any of those battles. I hadn't destroyed ships or killed an enemy I didn't know, or annihilated a political infrastructure foreign to me. That was yesterday, yet here I was preparing myself to defend against a new conflict in the Far East. This time, Vietnam.

The feeling left as quickly as it came, and I released the brakes. I was shoved back in my seat by a buzz saw propeller and angry engine cursing my delay. Flight deck elevator one raced by. At elevator two, I eased back on the stick. The nose lifted and the wheels left the deck just as the bow flashed beneath me. I slapped the landing gear handle up, listening for a thump as the wheels tucked away in the fuselage. Three green lights winked out confirming it. I was elated, having completed my carrier qualifications, but sad too, knowing Robert was gone. His life hadn't ended—I philosophized, just a new one beginning. The worry and pain were behind him now. I held altitude, letting the plane accelerate rapidly to 250 knots, then I yanked back hard on the stick. The plane lurched into a vertical climb and I held it there, trading speed for altitude. At 7500 feet I eased over into level flight and "joined up" on the other planes. We circled the carrier one last time, dipping our wings in farewell to a friend, then turned northeast for the flight back to Pensacola.

Why Robert and not me, I kept asking myself? Why had there been a switch in aircraft assignments? The answers still elude me. My friends commiserated with me, touched my shoulder, and told me that I had angels watching over me. Maybe each of us is born to a mission. For some it's completed early, for others, it takes years.

Most of us passed through the gate and became "true" Navy Pilots, entry into an elite group. As was the custom, we celebrated hard that evening, each in his own way. At first reliving wild memories of the day through embellished stories—one after another before drinking ourselves silly. We laughed. I smiled too, then cried. I couldn't escape the vision of Robert going "down." Were it not for the lady I had met hours earlier, I think I would have given in to the insanity of it. But she urged me away from the group and its stupor, driving me silently through the night to her home.

And for the rest of the evening we were madly in love. She unveiled her mystery, offering up a woman's sculpture and beauty that brought me to the moment of divinity. She, a mythical goddess in my mind. Me, a raging beast. But it was the softness of her skin that tempered me, as I guided my hands. And it was the smell of her body as I nuzzled my face gently down her belly, and the excitement of our tongues urging us on. She took me away. To the nirvana of her soul. To freedom, and a place I can never really remember, and yet, a place I will never forget. That momentary connection when you see God, where life is death combined in a paradox defying explanation.

The Board of Inquiry convened, reviewing depositions, including mine, as well as the departure film of Robert's final moment. In time they issued their findings, though I never saw the final opinion. I suppose forced insulation had its value and the pace of our instruction was too exhaustive for me to dwell on very long. Robert's memory settled into the recesses of my mind and his image blurred with the settling dust. But there were others, too, who joined him along the way. Fortunately for me, they were only familiar acquaintances from a distance. Six were gone in the first year of my training.

Sloppy acrobatics claimed one in front of his own family and friends and the public at Pensacola Beach. The student raced low across the bathers, then jerked the T-28 into an aggressive climb, then into a loop, but he was way short on altitude and dangerously slow coming over the top, he stalled and fluttered out of control, plummeting straight down like an albatross, diving into the ocean.

Another gone when an exhaust valve disintegrated, swallowed up by 18 runaway pistons. The pilot did an excellent 'dead stick' touchdown in a farmer's field until a deep culvert snagged the careening plane, snapping the student's neck.

Four more wiped away when fire broke out in the number one engine, and the wing burned away leaving four students and their instructor to cartwheel into the earth.

Then there was me, a neophyte aviator with less than 200 hours total pilot time trying to master a high performance fighter. I sat strapped in the beast, number three man in a flight of four plus an instructor, flying formation from NAS, New Orleans back to NAS Whiting Field. Somehow on that day, I survived the scythe of the Grim Reaper. How and why, I'll never know. Fate I suppose. Or, maybe it was just the maze I wandered through, that it was still being constructed and it led nowhere—not to heaven or hell, or to the boring delay of purgatory.

Puffy cumulus clouds dotted a turquoise sky a thousand feet above us while mustard-colored sand and forests of green pine trees dotted Florida's panhandle 7500 feet below. *Oh yeah, this is glory!*

Downwind and "dirty" for my first landing on an aircraft carrier, the USS Wasp.

Crossing the "Fantail," tail hook down and looking for a wire. In case the hook skipped a wire (called a "bolter"), we immediately applied full power maintaining our speed as we raced along the deck for another take-off, and, another attempt at "catching a wire."

Me with a demon machine, in 1969.

We left Whiting Field in September, 1969, to practice formation flying. Here is a typical tight parade formation; it takes intense concentration to maintain proper position on your wingman-two-feet of wingtip clearance and two-feet of step-down. Things were about to go wrong for me on the return leg.

Cockpit view of formation.

We moved into a "spread formation," I relaxed just a little, but that's when it happened-low fuel lights illuminating

Falling back and all alone, I thought, will I make it to the field?

I thought to myself as I tweaked the control stick maintaining a tight position on my wingman. "Piece-of-cake, WILLIAM!" I sang out over the racket of exploding exhaust and roaring slipstream ripping along the canopy. I was loving every second, but that's when it happened, *as it usually does*, when you are too relaxed and your guard is down, like being caged with a vicious animal and you turn your back for an instant forgetting the distance between the two of you. Then a swipe and tearing! A love tap if you're lucky—a bloody graze that brings you instantly back to reality as you roll to safety.

It bit me. I caught it out of the corner of my eye as I adjusted the trim wheels like a sailor making taut each of his sheets, guiding every puff of wind skillfully into his sails. An amber warning light illuminated suddenly with all the subtlety of a lightning bolt. I sat stunned, staring in disbelief, like a fool at the "LOW FUEL" lights. "It can't be!" I shouted, startled, tapping with my knuckles on the capsule like crazy, but the light wouldn't go out. "I had fueled in New Orleans." I looked right, then left, to see if I was siphoning fuel overboard. *Nothing! Clean wings! No! It has to be a bad gauge,* I reasoned . . . *this can't be happening. But the light is here for a reason, William! Think, God damn it! Think!!*

I checked the engine instruments. Sure enough, the blaring Curtiss-Wright was sucking gas as though someone had stuck a fuel hose directly into its guts. In a car, the gauge can read empty but there's still a 'dumb shit gallon' of gas remaining. In a plane they give you a light . . . which really says:

DEAR PILOT SIR:

BECAUSE YOU WERE STUPID TODAY, YOU NOW HAVE FORTY-FIVE MINUTES OF LIFE REMAINING.

BY THE WAY . . . YOU HAVE FIFTY-FIVE MINUTES OF FLYING TIME TO THE AIRFIELD. JUST THOUGHT YOU'D LIKE TO KNOW. THANK YOU. GOOD DAY!

OH, ONE MORE THING. WHEN YOU ARE FINISHED DIGESTING THIS MESSAGE, YOU WILL HAVE FORTY-THREE MINUTES FUEL REMAINING.

BYE FOR NOW!

I looked around for a gas station, naturally there wasn't one. And to survive I had to make up ten minutes of fuel in order to make the field. As I looked around the cockpit I suddenly recognized the problem. "OH MY GOD!" I hadn't leaned the engine out! I'd been pumping raw avgas (aviation gasoline) into 1425 thirsty horses for at least thirty minutes. And because of the sun's brilliance, I hadn't noticed the blue exhaust flame shooting down the cowling.

"Flight lead, from flight three!" I yelled into the mike.

"Go ahead, three."

"I've got a problem here. I have a low fuel light! I don't think I'm going to make Whiting. I'm breaking formation and slowing!

"Do not break formation!" he screamed back. "I repeat, do not break formation!"

"I have no option, Sir! I have to! I'm out!" I yelled, reducing power, easing my plane away from the flight. I watched, terrified as I have never been before, as the four planes dwindled into the distance, then became dark specks on the horizon. Fear mixed with panic scrambling from my gut to my heart and into my brain. I pulled back on the mixture lever until the engine coughed and nearly quit, then inched it forward slightly, mixing as little fuel as I dared with as much air as I could tolerate and yet keep the engine turning. I was totally alone now, not flying in one of the many training areas I had practiced in and memorized over the last few months. And there was no instructor to correct my mistakes or point the way to safety. It was up to me. I fought against erratic thoughts ricocheting like pin balls in my head. *I'm a dead man*, I thought. *Mom, Dad, I love you! I'm sorry! On this pristine day I'm going to die, not from illness, but from carelessness. I'll try for a dead stick on the interstate below.*

But every time I looked, the roadway seemed more crowded than before with weekend traffic. *Someone else is certain to go down with me if I try a landing there. No good!* I thought. *I can bailout! But . . . then the plane becomes a missile and there are homes and towns* . . . "SHIT!" My tongue felt glued in my mouth and my breath fouled by the 'last rites' of bile. Everywhere I looked the odds were against me. *If I do bailout now, the empennage* (the tail of the aircraft) *is sure to strike me, then, we both become missiles. No, no! I'll free my harness, roll inverted, push forward on the stick and catapult myself from the cockpit.* But the plane might change direction and explode in some home or business. Bad news again. "Damn!" *I'll have to ride it in. No choice but to continue on toward the field . . . jump or crash land. Right! Okay. Get as close to home plate as possible, then ditch.*

Every few seconds, I divided my attention between the fuel flow gauge, keeping the engine turning, looking for a place to land, holding heading and altitude, tuning radios, and navigating—all at the same time. I punched the sweep button on the clock timing my fuel burn per minute, then checked my ground speed, comparing and calculating how many minutes of fuel I had left and how far to the airfield. At my present speed I began overtaking the rate of burn—making up more miles per pound of fuel burned—to the point I thought I might just make Whiting. I breathed a sigh of relief but I was still in deep trouble.

Out in the distance I saw the inlet to Whiting. I retuned the radios; the needles jumped and pointed to where the field was located. But I felt I was closing on it at turtle speed. *Please engine, please keep turning!*

"Whiting tower, Navy Three, over?"

"Navy three, Whiting tower. Go ahead."

"Roger. I'm a 'T-Two-Eight,' twenty west inbound with low fuel . . . CRITICAL FUEL! Request a straight in."

"Roger, Navy three. Cleared to land any runway. Are you declaring an emergency?"

Well now, what do you think, you silly shit? Oh no! I'm just tooling around here on fumes and having a ball. Come join the fun! I wanted to say all this but merely answered, "Affirmative. Will land runway zero-five."

"You're cleared; trucks will be standing by. Call short final with the gear."

"Roger, Navy Three."

I'll take the approach high and fast, I told myself, *and if the engine quits I might still be able to glide to the field—if I can get close enough! Not pretty, but do-able.* I looked at the wind-milling propeller, "RUN BABY! RUN!" I willed and squeezed desire for life down from my brain through sweaty palms on the control stick out into the bowels of the engine. *You MUST sense my thoughts!* I nearly cried out, as if the engine had wisdom and feelings of its own.

Down I came from "high key," dumping out the landing gear and the flaps and speed brake. "NAVY THREE—GEAR DOWN!"

"Roger, Navy Three. Cleared to land."

Guess what? I'm landing anyway. I dove at the runway like a jumper off a skyscraper, totally without reason, but under the circumstances acceptable. My speed was too great and I risked overshooting the runway; *there might not be a second chance.* I kicked in rudder for extra drag and the plane nearly turned over on its back as I fought to correct it, but it slowed. Oh yeah, it slowed. The approach end of the runway flashed beneath me and I slammed the wheels onto the concrete. The screech of tearing rubber was like my soul being ripped free from an eternity of terror . . . like an executioner's bullet jerked to halt— only a millimeter from my heart—by an unknown force and falling harmlessly to the ground with a metallic clink. YOU HAVE BEEN GRANTED A SECOND CHANCE.

"Thank you, thank you! Thank you God!"

I taxied to the ramp and shut the engine down. For a moment I settled my head against the glare shield, breathing sighs of relief. But I still had to face my instructor. My future in aviation depended on his decision. Either I would continue flying, or, because of my stupidity, be banished to some cargo ship swabbing decks. I had no idea about the outcome.

I climbed from the cockpit on unsteady legs, teetered across the wing and slid down the flaps to Mother Earth. The plane looked as it always did, innocent yet menacing. Beauty and the Beast. How rude we humans are to make such creations *beautifully ugly*, and brutal.

An afternoon sun blazed red fire that barreled through the long flight line adding to the magic of the field—a place where we would-be aviators are allowed to mount our metal birds, then fly and jerk them brashly through the skies, like extensions of our own flesh.

My brush with death was over, but my confidence dribbled and oozed, staining my flight suit as black as the flood gates of fear had moments earlier. A row of T-28's stood parked in precise formation waiting patiently for a chance to claw at the sky. I looked on with envy as students I knew strapped themselves into their planes, while others busied themselves preparing their machines for flight. As I walked past them, all activity seemed to stop and heads whipped around in my direction. It was a chilling sensation, as if they knew something I didn't, like a window suddenly opened into my shattered soul, allowing voyeurs and the curious to gawk at my nakedness. I'm sure they enjoyed the wind spewing out holes in my blown-apart ego. *Thank God it's him that has to explain, and not me.* I could almost feel their thoughts.

I was too embarrassed to look back, but just kept shuffling the short distance to operations. They were the longest, loneliest, most dizzying steps of my life. Then I stopped for a second, turning to look at the plane that saved my life. *No! No!* "It was *me* who saved my life." *Please, never tell me how much fuel was left sloshing in those tanks.*

"What difference would it make anyway? I'm here."

At operations I recorded my flight time, signed the log book affirming there were no discrepancies with my plane, other than perhaps sludge coating the empty tanks. I slipped the metal jacket into its holder then stepped out to meet my fate.

At my instructor's door, I knocked the prescribed three times on the door jamb. "SIR! Ensign Leonard, reporting, SIR!"

"ENNERRRR!" Lieutenant Bebe's voice boomed through the walls.

Shit! *Here it is*, I thought as I opened the door and marched briskly to his desk.

"Sir!" I said, offering a sharp salute while standing at attention.

"AT EASE, Mister."

"Yes, Sir." I sighed, relaxing my weight, clasping my hands tight behind my back.

Seconds passed like minutes as he beat his fingers on my performance jacket, looking occasionally from it—to me—then back at the metal folder containing every hiccup, burp, and accolade in recorded Leonard aviation history.

"That little maneuver you pulled today jeopardized the entire flight. You exposed the formation to an opening that could have proved disastrous, one that an enemy could have used to his advantage in combat. You know that, don't you, son?"

What could I say except, "Yes, Sir . . . but uh . . ."

"But what, mister? That you saved your own butt and let your wingmen fend for themselves? Is that it?"

"No Sir, it's just that . . . well . . . we were not *in* a combat situation, my only choice was to slow and maybe make the field and save the plane. I don't see that I had any option, Sir. If I *had* continued at our present speed I was certain to run out of fuel, and possibly over a populated area. I thought what I did was right."

He didn't say anything for a few moments, just stood up and walked toward a window overlooking the flight line, now turned crimson by a falling sun. He tapped on the glass with his knuckles, then mumbled something I didn't understand.

"Sir?"

I watched as he rubbed the sides of his nose and jaw deep in thought, ignoring me. I was getting an uneasy feeling.

"You know," he said finally, resuming an annoying beat on the window. "Flying is easy. Anyone can do it. It's the decisions associated with it that are difficult, even gut wrenching. And that takes courage. What you did today . . . took courage, Mr. Leonard. I would have done the same thing. I'm not going to give you a 'Down,' although I should. What I am giving you is, a 'Below Average' in airmanship, and an 'Above Average' in head work. DON'T LET THIS HAPPEN AGAIN! UNDERSTOOD?"

"HELL YES, SIR! I mean, yes. Yes, SIR!"

"You've got a night flight tomorrow, Ensign. Don't screw it up. DISMISSED!"

"Yes, Sir!" I saluted, grabbed my tail and stuffed it back in my soaking flight suit; foul air raced behind me, competing with me for the door. I was too relieved to care, or breathe. Which I didn't. Not until that evening, and only with the help of John Courage and a six-pack of beer. I was a survivor . . . . But how and why?

My training continued and I struggled with the abstraction of flying blind on instruments with no reference to the ground. Somehow I got from point A to point B, smothered in clouds, relying entirely on compass cards, magnetic headings, tracks, radio bearings, navigation needles, sky waves and "E-hop-E" waves jiggling on the loran (a radio navigation display) screens, all of them trying to tell me which way to go. At times it was overwhelming, until I taught myself to relax. The day finally came. My family was there and my mother pinned Navy gold wings to my blue tunic. I was ready for Vietnam.

My training continued. Multi-engine flying and more carrier qualifications before receiving my wings and being assigned to a fleet squadron. I joined VW-One on Agana, Guam flying the Lockheed Super Constellation. We penetrated Typhoons all across the western Pacific, flying through these immense storms and towering wall clouds into the "eye." We did this at 500 feet off the water and at night. Shortly after that I was then re-assigned to VQ-One, the Navy's spy squadron, operating in the Gulf of Tomkin, Vietnam.

Dancing Through The Maze

SPOOK

How I came to be a spy, I don't know. Yesterday, I penetrated typhoons in the western Pacific, from the Mariana Islands to the Philippines, from Okinawa to Japan. And today? Today I'm a vicious hunter, stalking unsuspecting prey. That's operandi of my new squadron—Spy! Jam! Attack! I've gone from one terrifying nightmare to another, overnight. I guess I must be crazy like the others around me. No one told me that there were degrees of insanity, although the Flight Surgeon hasn't quantified me as thirty-three and one-third percent insane, or fifty percent nuts. But he has never flown into a 50,000-foot tidal wave—400 miles wide—swirling like an incensed ocean down a black hole, and in the middle of the night! That seems to satisfy the crazy category. Nor has he flown into combat as I'm about to, sneaking up the Gulf of Tomkin toward Hai Phong harbor and Hanoi in the dead of the night, slipping around phosphorus flares more brilliant than the Sun. This also seems appropriate for the insane folder.

I don't want to be here, yet, I am. Strapped tightly to my seat that moves in my aluminum cocoon at 350 miles per hour. I'm anxious and scared as we zip along teasing the black waves beneath us. It's like flying through a tunnel of love without the love. It's eerily peaceful, even quiet, if you discount the whining engines . . . the darkness is foreboding even with the flares. *What the hell am I doing Here? I just want to be an airline pilot, sip wine, fly to exotic safe places, make love.* Instead, here I am, a cloak-and-dagger spy.

49

Dancing Through The Maze

Even my plane is painted black to blend with the night. The cockpit instruments are barely legible in the dim glow of red lights. It's hot outside. Goddamn hot. My flight suit is soaking. I can taste the humid smells of Hanoi: its people, its pollution, its food, its life, the dampness of the surrounding rice fields and jungles.

I illuminate the radar for a quick check on my position, then shut it down so the "Gooks" can't lock me up. We're at the harbor now, moving north-northwest. I cinch my shoulder straps until my shoulders and chest ache. Not much longer now. *God, how I hope I live to see tomorrow.* My fingers strangle the control wheel at the thought of the anti-aircraft guns waiting to lay down metal clouds in front of us. I pray the Vietnamese are poor shots and that I don't go down in flames. Slamming into the Earth at over 400 miles per hour does not sit well with the connective tissue holding me together. And if I'm captured I don't want to humiliate my country. But I don't know if I can survive being crushed into a box half the size of a coffin before I convulse insane, or my mind implodes gasping for air. Either way I'm a dead man. I don't want to die, at least not here. If I have to go, let it be close to home where they can eulogize me properly, not dissect me from some rice patty.

The North Vietnamese are not supposed to know that we are here tonight, yet they do. Hanoi Hanna broadcasts our demise between pauses in western music:

"Good evening VQ-ONE," she addresses us politely. "Are you enjoying the music from your homeland? Do you have a request? No? Well no worry. This is your big night! Tonight you die. Remember your loved ones, and the horrific pursuit you perpetrate on the innocent peoples of Vietnam. Your jammers are useless against our radar guns. But you already know this, don't you? The Lockheed Constellation you fly is like a skyscraper with wings. There is no escape. You cannot hide. Enjoy the music because it will be your last. We choose the time. Good evening VQ-ONE!" Her tone is laced with sarcasm. *How in the fuck did she know we are here!*

"ANDY," I scream. "ARE WE RADIATING??!! KILL IT, NOW, IF WE ARE!!

"NO, Sir! We're passive."

"Time to target?"

"Five minutes," he replies.

"Everything secured?"

"All set, Sir."

"Standby the count!"

"RAINPROOF, RAINPROOF. THIS IS FATHER. ABORT, ABORT, ABORT. RAINPROOF, RAINPROOF. THIS IS FATHER. THIS IS FATHER. ABORT. RTB. RTB."

"Mr. Leonard? Did you hear that flash message: return to base?"

"I did. I'm turning right now. Hold on!"

We never really left South Vietnam that night. Just mounted our war birds and winged our way past imaginary elastic boundaries, that—when stretched thin—whipped us severely back to where we began.

Welcome to Hell!

Da Nang was burning when we arrived. I could see a billowing orange and yellow glow as we skimmed over "Monkey Mountain"—taking hits from small arms fire—before diving for the runway. I breathed a sigh of relief as the wheels kissed the concrete. "We made it!" *Yeah . . . until tomorrow comes.*

I taxied in silence, hypnotized into a blazing world. Lucifer's infamous island erupting now above the Earth's core. *His world.* Where fire sizzles like the fall of pounding hail, and smoke blocks the stars like raging black clouds. It was as though we were witnessing the death of a star in the faraway universe. I saw dead men walking in stupor through the flames. I saw helpless men offering riches for life. And I saw the ashes of their souls burst into flames, then settle like feathers to the ground. Hell *is Earth*, and war is a pathetic excuse for intellectual mass exorcism.

Dancing Through The Maze

Heading toward the fight. A twelve-hour mission over Hai Phong. One night Hanoi Hanna broadcast that she would shoot us down sometime that midnight. I had a measly .38 revolver strapped to my left shoulder. Super personal defense against MIG's and missiles.

, MONDAY, MARCH 16, 1970

22 Killed In S. Viet As U.S. Spy Plane Crashes

COPIED FROM WWW.NAVYCT.COM

One of two squadron planes lost in 1970. This one on touchdown at Da Nang. The other, shot down by the North Koreans.

TRANSITION

Richard called me today, to tell me my services were no longer necessary. He was firing me, although he didn't actually use those words, or put it in such direct terms. He said it has been an honor and that I should return home. That's how he put it. And when Richard Nixon speaks, people listen. I did. That's why I was here in the first place. When he invited me to the Far East, he gave me generous and considerate choices: the Army, the Navy, or the Air Force. There were two others that he didn't mention: Canada . . . or jail. I returned his call saying, "Hey Rich, thanks for the release. It has been my honor too, to kill, and maim, and disfigure the enemy (though I didn't realize I had any). But in order for me to leave, do you think you can stop the stream of lead and tracers from the 'Cong,' so I can run the gauntlet?"

"Billy . . . Billy . . . Billy . . . it's not my problem now!" he replied succinctly.

"Oh? Right! Okay. I get it." Then I said, "By the way Rich, I won't be needing the rubber valise you have with my name on it. You can give it to somebody else with my compliments. I'll find a way out of hell under my own power."

I never heard from Richard again. Not that I expected he would call. He and his buddies were busy in Paris. I understood this. The North Vietnamese were meeting with them over in France. But these crafty people roughed up Richie's boys in one of those dark alleys in the City of Love. Just like their "black clad army" was doing to us, back in Vietnam.

I climbed aboard my war machine one last time, lit the engines and set full throttle. Da Nang whizzed by as I circled, gaining altitude and precious momentum for my breakaway. Satisfied with the added speed, I turned east, taking aim on Richard's invisible political boundary. I flew down the sector's crimson corridor, straining to see the cobalt blue sky of freedom looming out in the distance. One more minute and I would leave forever the explosions, the moans, and the fires of hate. But would I ever be free from the screams for *mother*, the shouts for *wife*, or the cries for *children*? I gunned the engines pushing forward on the stick, diving hard for that extra impulse, then slashed my way through the "saran" of one man's belief, tearing through it like a Kamikaze. In a second—a heartbeat—I left behind the shrill volume of war and the tragedy of waste and its dying groans.

Things were not going well for Richie over in Paris. The French watched happily from the sidelines at all the spilled blood. And a worried Nixon raced to plastic surgeons to save his long face, but his jowls flapped like gelatin and the doctors couldn't stitch tight through gel. Yet we happy citizens tried to help, didn't we? Absorbing that horrific price? Nothing worked. How could it? It didn't work for Kennedy or Lyndon Baines, so why should it work for him?

I think someday I'll take the "Man" back to Ho Chi Minh City. Together we can tour the Cu Chi Tunnels, sip a Coke or a Pepsi, and wash down a Big Mac. It's quite the thing now. And even more astonishing, Hanoi Hanna says she wants to make love to me. My goodness! A heartbeat ago she spat lead at me. She hissed hysterically, sneering and clawing for my eyes. Now she's a kitten rubbing back and forth against me, anxious to purr. So this is what 58,000 body bags and two million dead Vietnamese have bought. What have any of us learned from all this? An intro lesson to capitalism? A chain of hotels, restaurants, resorts and red lights, tourism and trade. Welcome comrades in crime! To blood money. See beneath the table? Witness dollars whirling by and the smoke of fiery contracts being forged. Watch the souls of our brothers and sisters snatched away from salvation.

Richard Nixon spoke to me that one last time, and I listened again. But now I can't undress culpability that haunts me each day, every night that I live. It splashes into my brain like random drips from a water torture, raising clouds of dust that overlay my guilt. Those tautly curled tendrils of disgust. Each filament anchored deep in a fissure within my subconscious. When I read about war, I cry. When I dream about war, I shiver. When I make love to war, Purgatory laughs. Have I stained my soul and lost it forever? I'm at a loss for words and there is no one to comfort me.

There was no confetti at JFK airport, Long Island, New York, when I arrived. Just Mom and Dad, my brother, a few cousins to greet me, and a "welcome home" sign. That was it. No parade down the Belt Parkway, and no one quite knowing what to say to me. The nation was divided against the war and so was my family. Young people hated it and I suppose me too, for engaging in it. We drove along in awkward silence.

A lot had changed here in Brooklyn. More rust on the Verrazano bridge, a few more ethnics wandering the grey cracked sidewalks: Chinese, Indian, Pakistani, Israeli. Some of the avenues were crumbling in decay. Some of the streets were gouged with reconstruction.

But there was a tilt to Brooklyn I couldn't quite explain. Maybe it was just that the bricks and concrete seemed more tarnished and pale than I remembered. Four years of weather had taken a toll. But no. It was something else. Not just the punishment of scorching summer sun, or the pounding of rain and sleet on homes and office buildings. It was all that and more when taken as a whole. As if the city had ingested far more calories of clay and stone and tar than it could safely carry, or hygienically digest. Brooklyn seemed lethargic and choked, out-sizing itself in both height and girth.

Fourth Avenue was devoid of foliage and naked.

I'm still in Nam, and Brooklyn is like "Vin" and it has suffered an attack with a deluge of Agent Orange.

I can almost see the planes. Taste their exhaust. Hear the tankers ravaging the country-side with red dust. When the forest shrivels, dying in sadness, all that is revealed are more rolling hills. What have we accomplished?

My father turns away from the avenue's nakedness and the crawling jumble of traffic, accelerating onto 73rd street. My street. A street sheltered by a canopy of untouched trees hiding the sun, whisking us into sudden evening twilight. We drive on without caution. I press deep into my seat, secretly drawing back from silhouettes eager to take me down.

Where do I fit? I ride in comfort in the land of in-between, yet, still live in angry darkness. I've reviewed the evening's mission. Moved from bunker to the hanger. Painted myself like the night. Climbed into my blackbird and lit the fires. There is no escape.

Shafts of light cut down between leaves and tree limbs, flashing at me like pulses from a strobe. My eyes rest, but the light is intense and offers back a reminder.

I weave aggressively between phosphorus flares brighter than the sun. And I sweat, waiting for that hot thud of lead to strike.

We're less than a mile from my home and my father has to veer around a truck double-parked. A car rips out suddenly from the shadows. We barely miss hitting him as we swerve by.

I'm pulling "G's", lurching from a streaking missile searching for my wings.

"That was close," he says, as he steers back to the center of a ribbon of macadam that seems to have been poured from a huge cauldron in the sky. A black trail of thick sludge laid on the side of a hill, creeping down toward our home like lava. But the encounter rattles me. I've learned about suddenness *over there,* and its surprise always alarms me.

Nothing I do right now settles my racing heart.

What is going on here? Someone has surgically removed a sliver of my memory of Brooklyn. Injecting a syringe of morphine into my mind, numbing it, then purifying what remains of its contours and ridges with antiseptic, destroying all in its path: The warm memories of my youth, the churning passions of a teenager, the innocent loves fulfilling a young man. All cleansed and pureed into liquid, left to trickle slowly away. Run, Bill! Run!

"Honey? What is it? What's wrong?" My mother asks.

"Nothing. Nothing," I lie, wiping the sweat of fear from my face.

"Dad! Hold it! Stop! I'll walk the rest of the way."

"Why? What? We're nearly home," he says.

"I know. I just want . . . need to walk. All right?" It's not a question. My reply is tainted with acrimony and delivered without option. He realizes this and eases to a stop.

I pull up the handle and open the door. "I'll be there shortly," I say, leaning to get out. I see tears in my mother's eyes and confusion blinking in my father's.

"I'm okay, really," I tell them. "It's just, well . . . no, never mind. It's nothing. I'll be all right. The party can wait another few minutes. Right?" Then I close the door and walk. And wonder. And breathe in freedom. Yet, I have to run again. From the clutches of confinement and the black death of claustrophobia.

The offering waits for me, the returning victor, and it chills me. *Why Bill? Because there is no religion attached to it? Maybe. How can there ever be? Not after this. I'm left to wonder what God thinks of me, the vanquisher who has severed, broiled, flamed-to-cinders fellow humans, who once drowned in that wonder we call love. Seared strangers, who in humility invented our math, wrote our language, harnessed energy from this planet and walked proud like me. How comical it is, isn't it, Bill? Us. We intelligent creatures removed one step from animalism, dancing with the devil residing in us.*

War has altered and compressed my understanding of ethics and morality delivered so many years ago. Ideologies sent to me feather light, on carefully constructed waves of behavior, that is, until the last four years when they were destroyed ungraciously. Values set deep in my spine, immolated and gone forever. And all I ever wanted was the dream. To fly away. *So, Mother? Father? What do you think of this shell, now? Hmm?* I look at them and I see through them. They have become just . . . people. I've lost recognition. I'm supposed to love, but it vanishes in confusion.

They want back their yesterdays. To ride smiles against time, hoping my life will give them reason and substance, to live through the paradox of present and past co-joined and copulating like lovers. It's all there for them, wrapped and tucked neatly in each falling second. They don't see that war has destroyed my backward glance, my confidence in life distorted. I've broken God's laws like Moses, so what's left, Bill? What is the remainder?

I grit my teeth. Inhale for strength. Continue walking toward home, *their* home. *I'll fumble through duty of fete.*

Voices come at me echoing like groaning winds swept through a canyon. Sounds with meaning I suppose, from faraway lips. They strike at my flesh but don't reach the core, that tributary of innocence, disfigured and slashed away by the cries of mothers and fathers, watching loved ones melt away. All of that energy and heart gone to eternity. Such waste. *My God!*

So the voices of cousins and family speak to me, even ask, but their words ricochet off my numbed mind. I haven't come back. Not yet, at least.

For a few weeks I languished, trying hard for the transition, but the buffer was too loose and too diffuse. The loneliness growing more intense as seconds fell like hours, and days turned like years. There was nothing to love. The bar scene, a way station of agony, though its trough of alcohol a refuge.

Each day I hunted—work for protein and sustenance, women for validation to soothe the ache of my distorted world. The routine settled in, seemingly taking on its own personal form. In daylight, I searched the want-ads hoping for a job, and in the night, sniped bars, longing to inhale the perfume of a woman's affection. I held my breath as the Earth turned farther and farther away from the sun.

Flying is a unique profession, and openings for such positions were severely limited, particularly with the glut of other returning pilots from Vietnam, like myself.

One day I saw a small ad in the employment section of the *New York Times*. An upstate commuter airline was looking for pilots. It wasn't the majors, but it was a way back into the sky, a stepping-stone. A refuge from emptiness. I called and sent a resume.

A few days later they invited me for an interview.

Dancing Through The Maze

CIVILIAN

Poughkeepsie, New York. *Where the hell is that? In Canada? Near Buffalo?* I traced my finger up a road atlas of New York State, starting at the south/southeastern corner of New York—at the Narrows River, that small body of water buffered between the Hudson River and the Atlantic Ocean. It separates Brooklyn and Long Island from mainland U.S.A. I searched geographic grid S-22 for Poughkeepsie, that's where the legend said the town was located. Later, I learned this was also IBM country.

Poughkeepsie is a town of reasonable size just off Route 9, but hard to drive into because of poorly sequenced traffic signals. Its other claim to fame, though, is prestigious Vassar College.

The interview went reasonably well. They asked only a few general questions. My replies were truthful. I told them, "I'm here for experience, not the money. When a major airline calls, I'm gone." They couldn't argue against logic. But they did have a need and I easily filled the requirements. A few days later I was hired as a First Officer. I'd be flying fifteen-seat propjets out of Dutchess County Airport.

Freedom returned, and along with it—peace, which is what I needed right now. Sounds of nature floated like lyrical notes in the air, caressing me, lifting me up.

I drove north, watching Brooklyn fade in the rear view mirror. There was an edge of sadness and selfishness dragging on my heart as I said my goodbyes. A feeling that comes with understanding and regret. I was leaving home again, the way I did for college and for war. Heavy mist fell like teardrops, trickling down the back window as though it could wash away my sentiment. But that could never happen.

There were more dues to be paid. For whatever reason a pause was necessary. The maze held on tight, not giving up its secrets so easily. It kept me secure though, yet off-balance. The groove of my future, still too rough and unpolished for my well-being. Nothing in it right now was so awe-inspiring for me to say, "I've found nirvana and must drive home a stake." Few of us ever make that remark. I was no settler in a brave new world.

Maybe the delay was warranted. Having something to do with maturity. *Perhaps.* But riding above the earth through capricious weather at warp speed, dragging innocent people with their own rich histories and poignant lives negated such an unjustified thought.

"Take a break Bill; park here for awhile," the maze seemed to say. "Poughkeepsie looks good from this perspective, don't you think?"

What could I say? Did I even have an option?

I had been living in a world of narrow vision the last four years. The Navy's world. Where rigid flying was a stunted indoctrination into the marvels of flight. That was all I knew.

We were tasked to execute aerial drills in an unreal sheltered world. Only a thin veil separated combat flying from what I believed to be the more gentle grace of commercial flying. But there is ruthlessness even there—in that big boy arena tied to the whims of Wall Street.

In the Navy I learned to fly in a "don't ask questions world." We flew in a restricted course, not far from the airbase, learning how to dominate an opponent. Being gentle was not a consideration. They taught brawn. It was you . . . or him. Survival is a nasty business. We mastered tricks to ensure that we could, invented others for a merciful coup-de-grace. The "Brass" told you how to fly. They didn't ask. "Fly it our way, or it's no way!" They said. "Get it?"

So we accepted and prepared ourselves for the lunacy of war. *Time* certainly was a factor, but not nearly as critical as it is in civilian aviation.

The one common denominator between the two was money. Is the investment worth the risk?

Command Airways was no exception. As nations drew closer with the explosion of technology and the spread of capitalism across the globe, evils came: competition, an insatiable quest for power, mistrust, animosity, greed, and the ever present stirrings toward war. *Unstable fission poised for one huge bang.* Command struggled in this battlefield, investing its soul in the turmoil. And we naive pilots offered them ours.

Command was a small company operating on frayed threads, boasting glory emblazoned in local newspapers, and its hype playing in jingles on the radio—beaming throughout the Hudson Valley. People accepted this with confidence, never knowing the whole truth. But glitter is no lubricant. Command's planes were tired and groaned from punishment. They were fifteen-seat machines with limited range, old avionics for navigation, and no autopilots to relieve stress and fatigue.

It was a rude awakening for me here. A let-down from all the sophistication and high power machinery I was used to flying in the Navy. All I could do was to look upon this as another path through the maze. *Welcome to the real world, First Officer Leonard.*

Dancing Through The Maze

COMMUTER FLYING

The trade was mutual: my tan Navy uniform, for a black one; gold stripes that once draped my shoulders, for silver; light brown shirts for more sophisticated, white. And the tie? Thinner, but still a boring black. Gone too, were the salutes. Except now from linemen, but even they were less accurate than those in the Navy. The transition was nearly complete, although the drapery merely a shell. It was as fragile as a chrysalis. But that's how I looked that June of 1972, standing in front of one of Command Airway's airplanes. *How do I paint freedom? Can I gloss it with color? Does it even matter, Bill?*

From my first day at Command, I knew this could never be my home. It was just another experience in a growing list branded into my flesh. Another chapter in an unfolding story. Years of a blazing sun could never alter it. Rains and wind would never erode it. *We are the scents . . . and we are the essence of what is to be.*

I found a small apartment outside town, not too far from Vassar college, and one block off the main drag. The third floor of a three-family home. There was no door bell for my apartment, so I rigged my own. Anchored a bell inside the small kitchen and attached it to batteries. Wires snaked out the window, down to a throw switch at the front door. Next to it was a plastic bag, with a message: "If you need me, throw the switch. Don't let it ring too long! And don't forget to turn it off, or you'll kill the batteries!" The plastic bag protected the card from the weather, so I wouldn't have to keep re-writing it. But there were never many rings. My new home. Bachelor pad extraordinaire: a cot, some dishes and utensils, a few cherished books, and above all else, my prized stereo.

A few days later, after a ridiculous ground school (the FAA would have shut us down had they known), I was off flying the "line," immersing myself deep into a twisted rollicking apprenticeship as a "commuter pilot."

Command flew air taxi flights with four aircraft. Two lumbering DeHavilland Twin Otters, and two much faster Beech 99's. The Otters, with fixed landing gears and wing support struts, were slow. Their burly design fought engine thrust as unwelcome drag. They were good machines though, particularly for heavy lifting, or operating in rough terrain. I preferred the Beech-99, with its retractable landing gear and excellent aerodynamics. And it was very fast for a propeller airplane. Either machine was good in the weather; both could fly with a heavy load of ice.

Our flight schedule was limited to: New York metro airports; Binghamton, New York; Burlington, Vermont; and Boston, Massachusetts.

It was a crazy domain at Command. Passengers crammed into seats translated into greenbacks, and greenbacks into a paycheck and another day of nourishment. We escorted the passengers to the planes, slung their bags into the cargo hold, buckled them in, and chugged them to wherever the tickets said they paid to go.

"Air taxi," that's how we were originally described. An appropriate title for the era we were in. We flew these planes like New York City cabbies barreling through a crazed concrete jungle. The FAA chose to ignore our brashness, even tolerated our boldness.

We trained in looseness, partied with abandon, flew fearless below weather, when at times, we should have been flying locked on the gauges, flying bull's eye into the cat's eye. Some days we did, piloting hour-after-hour in intense tedium, staring at instruments as we sped through a day of endless clouds, rain, ice, and snow.

I thought I knew radio navigation, the way I was taught in the

Navy: after all, I held a commercial pilot's license with an instrument rating. But it didn't compare to the knowledge I gained flying at Command.

We became extremely proficient at radio navigation, making our "out-classed" planes race when they were designed to jog. Particularly, when we had to fly behind huge jet airliners as we struggled to hold altitude in their wake, yet, nail an inbound course without deviation, straight to the runway. And how the engines took this punishment is a testament to Pratt and Whitney. The constant jockeying of the throttles and wild swings in internal temperatures (engine killers), yet, they kept turning. We had to match speed with arriving jets, or be ripped from the sequence because we were too slow. And this meant another fifteen minutes vectoring through the weather with low fuel. So we pushed our planes and demanded even more power from the engines, trying to avoid such situations.

We gained an enviable reputation as "can do pilots" by the New York Air Traffic Controllers. That meant they could count on us to do just about anything, and still keep their arrival flows moving. Which we did.

Most days we flew VFR (visual flight rules) snaking down the Hudson River, hiding beneath dark nimbus clouds trying to stay on schedule. We'd cut across White Plains and Rye, then Long Island Sound toward Kennedy Airport. Not only did it save time, but it eliminated a year's worth of stress. I didn't have to rely solely on the flight instruments if we suddenly found ourselves hidden in clouds. Ground reference alone, was all we needed.

In just under six months at Command, I became a Captain. I settled comfortably into the routine, but never turned my back on anything. I dissected the words of my dispatcher, my Chief Pilot, even the meteorologists for any loophole in their messages. It was little things that could get you killed. Murphy's Law. "If something can happen, then it certainly will." I doubled checked everything!

The Hudson River became my friend, a navigation aid, and a life saver. Every twist and bend was etched into my memory. I could tell the month of the year just by the color of landmarks on its shores. We knew the surrounding hills and sometimes used them to an advantage as we raced between their saddles. And we knew where high tension lines swept across the slopes waiting to snag us from the sky. All of this, because of an incessant race against time. Time was money! It became a credo and an enemy.

It was "good time" if wind was on your tail, and "bad time" when it switched around pressing against the plane's nose. They could be capricious though, sometimes one hundred-eighty degrees out from a forecast.

Time could make you fuel, or rob it from you. *Time!* It became anchored in my psyche for my entire career. I lived life by its tick. By the innocuous sweep of hands around a dial.

At Command you had to stop by the flight clinic for your daily injection of the 'creed' (beat the clock juice) before mounting the bird.

The suits gave you a machine, pointed the way, then shot you skyward. Dollars fluttering through the sky after you. But, where was the money when we argued the planes needed maintenance? Or, that we needed better avionics to fly such a demanding schedule. Management would nod, agreeing with us. But as was the case, we had to wait months for replacement parts. Yet, we drove these planes as though they had just left the factory.

How this was all accomplished depended upon the depth of acquired knowledge imbedded in a pilot's soul; his status with the company, the grey in his hair, and the plane he was assigned, and yes, his position in the maze. The public never felt the buzz—the tension, all they saw were the stripes sewn on your sleeves, so they believed.

Management looked through us and into the air transport industry with tunnel vision. For them, all that mattered were figures written in ledgers and the number of dollars remaining in the register. It was brutal competition. And for us, a daily war of survival. We were the front line.

Command took me places many would envy, while others would cringe because of the life/death struggles. Those unexpected—out-of-nowhere—nerve shattering battles with the "Grim Reaper."

It seemed to happen at least once a year. A blindsided attack when you were too relaxed and unfazed with life. A smack of humility against a rosy cheek. The battle-ground always the same—a barren knoll. We combatants bowing to one another in respect, assuming our positions of ferocity, preparing for assault. We slashed and lashed out at one another, parrying for advantage. Sometimes the fight would end quickly, in a flurry of chops. Other times it dragged on for hours. Yet, somehow I was always able to pick myself up, though wounded, and back away. Neither of us claiming victory.

I survived frozen throttles—not unlike a car's accelerator getting stuck against the floorboards and the vehicle racing out of control. We were heading toward Dutchess County Airport one day, at full speed, unable to move the throttles to slow ourselves. There was no choice but to shut an engine down in order to land. When I brought the propeller into full "feather" and shut off the fuel, the engine nearly snapped away from the wing. But we made it. Hearts pounding, but home.

Another time, on landing, a propeller slapped into reverse while the other didn't. We shot off the runway slicing down through the grass and into the weeds. Somehow the landing gear stayed intact and we walked away.

There were two crashes, fortunately not mine. How my friends survived either of these, I'll never know. Not when I viewed the twisted wreckage.

Once a year you'd do battle in the air.

I suppose that's why we tried so hard for love at Command, to temper living on the edge. I craved a woman's soothing caress. *That certain touch only a woman's delicateness can offer. How fortunate they are. Beauty always there for them. Whether in the velvet of their hands or in the sweetness of their lips. Simply being. What awesome power. A woman's understanding and patience offered as*

a guide, whisking you from harshness to that marvelous world of lingering warmth. Their affection magical. Opening dimensions where time is suddenly a friend, and days no longer have names. A woman's love, bringing reason and focus.
For all of them . . . I am thankful.

There were many lady friends I came to know in Poughkeepsie. Some I'd bring along on evening flights—cargo flights, without passengers. I'd let them sit in the co-pilot's seat, watching them marvel like children as we slid across the earth, balanced effortlessly beneath a breathtaking canopy of glowing stars. This was my love, my magic world to share with them.

I introduced this art to one special woman in particular, her name—Lucinda (Cindy), and whisked her breathlessly up into my domain, offering her that secret part of me living in a third dimension. A world that defies any attempt at explanation. A world of color to some, when lived so long in years of black and white. You see it there as I did, in those wide gleaming eyes, drawing in every second of sorcery and beauty from passing space. And me, sitting there on a throne of power like a little boy—giddy, thrilled to share my "Peter Pan world."

I watched Cindy's every move as she etched each marvelous sparkle of this dizzying panorama deep into memory. *How fortunate am I to have two loves. Do you believe me now, when I tell you I am in love with you? And with my life here, in a land of illusion?*

Her answer wasn't necessary. She was gone. Enthralled as we rode along that seductive cushion of invisibility, that one of mystery, supporting the grace of man's wisdom and his creation.

We did this on a few other opportunistic occasions. Then we decided we should share this elegance uninterrupted—forever.

It was a beautiful evening wedding, dancing to the glow of candlelight and the intrigue of melodies from a harpsichord. The stars shimmered like diamonds that cold January evening. They still do.

Things actually improved for a while. Command purchased new

fifty-seat airplanes, and I was the first Captain to fly one. Suddenly our company became a "Regional Airline." We felt proud of the growth. But there were no real changes to the daily operations. Pay was still woefully poor, no benefits or a retirement package to look forward to. Nothing here for me, except experience and another day's entry into a thickening log book.

During those five long years, I never stopped applying to major airlines. Some of them would call me, and I'd take their three or four-hour "Stanine" exam, talk with psychologists to see how sane I was, then fly a simulator under scrutiny. In the end I always seemed to lose out to the "jet jocks." But one of those psychologists lost out, too. He became fed up with living and listening and talking, taking his own life. Maybe I didn't want to work at his company after all.

I knew I needed "pure jet" experience, so I applied to the Veteran's Administration for educational money for such training. It was a long drawn-out process.

In the interim, I left Command, taking another position as a Captain flying in the South Pacific.

Things were much more relaxed in Samoa, as expected. South Pacific Island Airways had a mixed fleet of small planes: one Twin Otter; two Cessna Four-Twenty-ones and one Tri-Islander.

The Otter was a 300 series and more sophisticated than Command's DeHavillands. It was set up for over-water flights with better navigational aids and high frequency radios.

We flew to Eastern Samoa, the island of Ofu, the Kingdom of Tonga, and the Vava'u group of islands. Mostly bringing supplies, but tourists, too, who needed an infusion of reason, and a place to put life on hold. It was a journey back in time.

Grass huts sitting on poles to capture cool breezes, native men and women with tattoos and grass skirts, outrigger canoes for fishing, and those lush green mysterious mountains we flew around. Many times we landed in the heart of dense forests, on narrow coral strips cut through the trees. I always wondered what ferocious beast might rush us from such dark walls of vegetation. But it was always the

Dancing Through The Maze

COMMAND AIRWAYS PLANE RESTS IN FIELD ACROSS FROM DUTCHESS COUNTY AIRPORT

Poughkeepsie Journal Photo by Robert V. Niles

Commuter flying. It was a tough business. I was in a holding pattern this stormy winter's day in 1975, when my friends took off. They barely made it airborne, when the weight of ice and slush brought them down, just beyond the end of the runway, and across a two lane roadway. I was running very low on fuel and made a desperate landing. I ran to the crash site. How anyone survived is a miracle. The Captain did a great job. The only serious injury was to the First Officer. Just a week earlier, this same gentle hill had been cleared of trees.

An Accident Prevention Award I received from the FAA in 1976.
John Karp of the FAA presents the award to me; next to me is my First
Officer Ben Conklin and Command's Chief Pilot Sid Richardson is at far
left.

One of Command's new fifty-seat SD3-30's built by Short Brothers Har-
land of Belfast, Northern Ireland.

73

villagers who came.

The Chief would greet us, host a ceremony, as though we were gods descending from the clouds. We ate and we drank. A festival before flight. He forbade us to leave until we indulged. We were careful to obey him. It was a weekly event with its own protocols. I swear there must have been a narcotic in that brown ceremonial water. How I ever took off remains a mystery to me, even today. I think we flew back in long graceful and carefree arcs.

But, reality from home struck one day. The death of a parent—my mother. *Part of Gibraltar cleaving, sliding into the sea.* So I returned to New York to grieve.

BACK FROM THE SOUTH PACIFIC

We moved back upstate—to Poughkeepsie, while my father packed his few belongings, then left Brooklyn for the warmth of Florida. Crazy, each of us looking for a new start. So we scattered, because it was necessary for us, and also for my father. We moved along separate, yet parallel paths. Youth and age. Each weaving deeper into the fabric called life, looking for individual ways to continue the process called living. His image faded with my daily routine. I'm sure mine did too, in his eyes.

There were many jobs after Command and my short stay with South Pacific Island Airways. For a while I took temporary work driving a truck instead of an airplane, delivering freight up and down the lower Hudson valley. This went on for a time, though I never stopped scouting regional airports for flying jobs.

Just one more delay in the maze, I figured. In desperation, I used some of my own money to attend Lear Jet Ground School.

A charter company in Teterboro, New Jersey said they would hire me, but only if I satisfied FAA requirements for the type of jet they operated. So, it was back to another school. And two weeks later, true to their word, Teterboro Aircraft Service put me on the payroll. I began flying the Lear, but also the twin turbo-prop Merlin, and the Cessna 421. The pay was good, but the drive from Poughkeepsie at all hours, a strain. I located an apartment close to the airport. Another separation from my home, but we needed the money. The charter business was picking up and I flew most days—Florida,

Virginia, Massachusetts, Pennsylvania, and the Bahamas.

A few months later, the V.A. wrote that I had been approved for educational money. I immediately applied to the United Airlines Flight Training Center to obtain a Captain's rating on the Boeing 737. However, the instructors there warned against coming. "Don't waste your money," they said. "This school is very intense, even for United's own experienced pilots. It would be almost insurmountable for anyone who has never flown a large jet."

The usual path toward a "Captain's seat" with an airline requires many years experience as a Flight Engineer and as a First Officer, although now, the engineer position has been eliminated, just as the Navigator and Radio Operator positions were. Ten years flying as a Co-Pilot (Second in Command) is not unheard of. But ultimate authority and responsibility resides with the "left seat." I was asking for a Captain's rank though I had never touched the controls of such a large and complicated airplane. "Think twice about this," is all they could say. But they had their careers, I reasoned to myself. I needed to be more competitive.

I listened as they tried to dissuade me, but ultimately told them I was willing to accept the risks. Naval flight school after all, had not been a picnic either.

My Chief Pilot at Teterboro Aircraft Service was a wise man and understood the trappings and lure of the sky. He knew the difficulties I faced, trying to forge a pathway into a dream. He had stumbled down a similar road many years before. I respected him for what he still held on to so dearly, at his age. I saw it blazing there, in youthful gleams sparkling off his intense brown eyes, and the pleasing sweep of crow's feet set across his tan-weathered face. A true birdman living life to its fullest on the wing. We bid our farewells with a firm handshake.

It was not easy saying goodbye to my wife. I was leaving on another mysterious journey into the unknown. I left for Denver, anxious and even a bit apprehensive. There were no assurances out west. *Have I taken on something well over my head? Even if I complete upgrade training and earn a Captain's rating, United is in no position to offer me a job.* They made that clear. I would have to re-apply through United's corporate offices. That meant back to ground zero, starting over like thousands of other applicants. *Are their dreams any less important than mine?*

There were no misconceptions about the school. It was tough. A firehose of information and testing smothering my brain. Each day, a new system with complex schematics committed to memory and my desperate hope for fluid understanding. Testing the next day followed by yet another system. Day after day, the regimen continued. I studied late into the night with little sleep. Two weeks of hell rolled by, then a long final exam. You had to pass the written before being allowed to take the extremely compressive and demanding "oral exam." A one-on-one sparring to prove your mastery of every switch, light, system, and instrument in the cockpit. Three hours of battle. But the hard work paid off, and I passed with top grades. I didn't have enough money to repeat any one section had I failed. I moved to Phase Two—flying the simulator.

Actually this was easy for me. My instrument experience at Command proved invaluable, and I breezed through the syllabus and check ride.

Finally, it was time to fly the actual airplane. All we were allowed was just one training flight. A midnight flight at Denver's Stapleton Airport. There were five of us on board, and a United Airlines Check Airman supervising. For three hours we each took turns doing "touch and go's" and single engine approaches. I loved it, it was a thrilling evening. The next night would be the final check ride. Again in the airplane, only this time under the watchful eyes of an FAA Examiner and the Check Airman from United. But it would be the FAA making the final determination as to "pass or fail."

This too was an easy ride for me, and I was awarded a Captain's certificate on the Boeing 737. No one could ever take that away from me. It was a powerful statement on my resume.

I immediately applied worldwide for a flying position.

Singapore Airlines did offer me a job as a Captain flying the French Airbus A-310. But it meant living in Singapore, half way around the world. And I would be an expatriate under contract, which was only good for two years. There were no guarantees the contract would be renewed. For me, that was too tenuous. I could be on the street again, a little older, competing against another group of younger aggressive dreamers. The offer was very tempting but I turned it down, setting my sights instead on an airline career right here at home.

My jet training and persistence was beginning to pay off, though. Corporate flight departments looked more closely at my qualifications and a few offered me jobs. There were a number of them: Ingersoll Rand, Volkswagen of America, and Texaco Oil Company. All top-notch conglomerates flying elegant executive machines. But there was a big drawback. You were on call all the time and tied to a pager. Family and social life became secondary. I accepted a position with Texaco, but only for the experience.

It was no secret that the major airlines offered excellent pay and benefits, and above all else, a schedule. No more uncertain days waiting for a call and a mad dash to the airport. No more endless long hours sitting in boredom, waiting for executives.

Then finally, eleven long years after the Navy and over five-thousand hours in the air—a break.

Some of my friends from Command had been hired by a new upstart airline—People Express Airlines, flying out of Newark, New Jersey. They were flying Boeing 737's, which I already held a "type" certificate in. I sent a resume and a cover letter requesting an application. A week later I received it, typed it neatly that very same day, and had it back into the mail by late afternoon. I made sure to reference my friends already flying at "Express."

Two weeks later I received another letter from them. This time it was an invitation to Newark, for an interview. I was ecstatic. An opportunity of a lifetime! It was scheduled for the following month, and that gave me ample time to research the company and prepare myself.

I wrote flash cards for every conceivable question the interviewers might ask. I rehearsed day after day, building up my delivery and confidence. My wife and I walked miles going over and over the questions. I wanted this job more than anything and couldn't imagine what direction my life would take if I wasn't hired. A defining moment in my life. Our lives. My body buzzed with anticipation. During that agonizing wait I organized my log books, scouring them to insure they were in impeccable order, that every minute of all my flight times were accurate, totaled, and up to date. If they should ask, I could easily defend every hour aloft, and describe in detail every plane I ever flew. And there were many: the Navy Beechcraft T-34, the Navy North American T-28, the Navy Lockheed, EC-121, the Beechcraft BE-99, the DeHavilland Twin Otter, the French Falcon 20, the Learjet 23 and 35, the Bombardier Challenger CL-600, the Gulfstream G-II, and the Short Brother Harland SD-30.

For security and easy access, I placed my Commercial Pilot's license, my First Class Medical certificate, and my Radio Telephone license into a protective clear plastic pouch. These documents would be checked and verified first on the day of the interview. Weeks dribbled by. Finally, the last Sunday of the month came. Monday would be the interview. I was ready.

Dancing Through The Maze

LIFE-PART TWO
THE MAJORS

Dancing Through The Maze

THE SURPRISE

There comes a time of times . . . perhaps today. Maybe this very moment, when a long ago vision and childhood dream is realized.
Thirty of us walked down a long brightly lit corridor toward a room set up like a classroom, rows of chairs neatly arranged in front of a bland wooden desk. Thirty of us dressed to kill. Some looking more like high-powered executives than pilots, freshly tailored in enviable fabrics as though ushered here from exclusive Madison Avenue tailors. Others dressed less extravagantly like myself—roughly hewn pilots in three piece suits provided by none other than Sears. A few of them sauntered by, cocky, armed with alligator attaché cases complementing their silk suits. Many eased in with scuffed-up leather flight bags adorned with decals of the jets they had flown. Vanity for all to see, flagrantly whipping these rich leather bags in front of us, like peacocks raising feathers. I looked on with envy, though. All I carried was a stack of beaten-up log books—my life's story secreted under cover. We chose our seats carefully, nervousness showing on our faces as we mentally measured the competition. *Who of us will get the nod and be hired today?*

There was little to do except wait and sit, clammy in our own self-generated humidity.

They came to us a little after 9 a.m., dressed in tailored brown Captain uniforms, four dark brown stripes circling the cuffs of their sleeves. Impressive, I thought.

83

They were polite and enthusiastic representatives of an exciting and wholly different type of airline. A hard-charging company buzzing off the front pages of Wall Street newspapers. Their amazing accomplishments echoing down the halls of Harvard Business School and throughout powerful banking firms and high profile brokerage houses.

"Welcome to the People Express Airlines Pilot Interview Session. I'm Captain Brown," he said, introducing himself, then his colleagues. "We thank you all very much for driving so far on this hot day, and to those of you who have flown in from so many different parts of the country to be here.

"As you may well know, we are a unique company in the airline industry, and growing. Each person here at Express is instrumental in that success. We are multi-tasked, which is our uniqueness. For some of you, this may seem foreign. But believe me, you are not just simply a pilot or flight attendant here at Express. You are a dispatcher, scheduler, ticket agent, operations manager, etc. Jobs that keep any airline in the forefront of the public eye—we work for *them,"* he paused a second for effect. "And we work for each other. We are *all* teammates."

The supercilious speech, I thought to myself. Every company I ever applied to thought they were the end-all, the best in the industry. *I just want an airline job! God, can't you see that, Captain Brown? I'm here because I want to fly your wonderful jets and then be left alone to my own adventure. I want to get my life on track. I've waited too long. Cut the pep talk. Let's get on with it!*

"Today, you will not be judged solely because of your piloting skills; that is a given, or you would never have been invited here in the first place. People Express needs your expertise and talent to help manage its continued growth. Each man and women plays an integral role running and streamlining this amazing organization. As I mentioned, you are here for that very reason, your multi-talented experience. You have been selected from an enormous pool of highly qualified applicants. We will be looking closely at your managerial skills." When he said that there was a buzz as we looked around at one another. I couldn't remember a company I actually managed, except in the Navy, and that was years ago when I was in charge of the Classified Material Control Office. I remember including that on my application. I had single-handedly consolidated, reorganized, and integrated procedures for collection and dissemination of secret material for two of the Navy's spy squadrons. *Maybe that's what they saw on my application.* I shifted in my chair, uneasy with all this. *Come on man! Get to it!*

Everyone around me seemed engrossed by this rah, rah, horn blowing. *First-timers, but not for me.* My hands had a mind of their own as Brown spoke, straightening the creases in my pants, fumbling with my shirt collar and tie, drying sweaty palms discreetly on my jacket, sneaking a hand up my face, wiping at beads of wet fear dotting my face. *The moisture of wicked thoughts from the dark recesses of my mind—fear of another rejection. I hope Brown can't read the look. The, I-haven't-been-hired-before look. Maybe he will see it? A character flaw all other companies must have seen in me, for one reason or another. What character flaw? Is he so perfect? Are any of us perfect? Seven times I've been here, in similar situations. Seven failures.* That look of defeat fought for expression on my face. I shifted in my seat, moving in my best attempt at camouflage, trying to look impassive, yet attentive. *But it's my damn eyes—they betray me with too much sensitivity. Please not today!* I heard Captain Brown's voice rise in the hollows of my mind.

"Our selection criteria becomes more critical at this stage, particularly in view of the limited number of positions we will be filling.

"Gentlemen, let me outline the process. First, there will be a written test, not the 'Stanine' you may be familiar with given by other companies." *Thank you God! Salvation from that shitty, four hour, grueling, and insane exam!*

"Ours *is* pointed, but not nearly as time-consuming. Interviews will begin shortly thereafter, and based upon test scores and the initial 'three-on-one interview,' some of you will be asked to return this afternoon for a final 'one-on-one' interview. The others will be free to leave with our thanks and deep appreciation.

"There will be a one hour break for lunch. Good luck to all of you. Are there any questions?" His gaze swept across the room.

"No? Then please follow me."

I don't remember much of what took place, it may have happened in staccato, though it seemed more like a slow motion journey through one diffuse cloud after another. The test covered math and English, and the three-on-one interview was more of a banter session, pleasant discussions of my accomplishments and my background. It was cordial. Two of the Captains were ex-Navy pilots. We shared tales of Vietnam, ships we flew off of, the training Command at Pensacola, and my present Reserve commitment. Naturally they were interested in Command Airways, and South Pacific Island Airways. I can only assume my test scores were satisfactory. At the end, I was asked to return for the one-on-one interview later that afternoon. My friends had warned that this first battery was crucial. Many perspective candidates would be eliminated right there. So, I was thrilled thinking I was still in the running.

I went to lunch, choked down some food, roamed the hallways a bit, then ambled back to the room at the appropriate time.

There were only fifteen of us now. I didn't see Mr. Madison Avenue, maybe he was just running late, I thought. Or perhaps he was needed back on Wall Street.

It began again at 1:30 p.m., not 1:00 p.m. as they had said. The cordiality of the morning vaporized in a sudden about face onslaught.

They called my name, but this time the interview was laced with tension and frenetic pressure. The interviewer—another Captain—introduced himself curtly, asked me to sit, then launched right into very incisive questions. They came at me as though shot from a gun. Bam! Bam! Bam! No sooner would I reply to one, when he lashed out with another.

"Let me ask you . . . why do you want to work here?

"Why Express and not someplace else? Where they require less work?

"Where you can 'laze' around? Hmm?" he shot back, as though he hadn't heard my reply.

"And why so many jobs in the past? I noticed quite a few here on your resume. Tell me about them.

"Ever been fired?

"Can we rely on you in view all these changes? Is there some problem you have with authority, perhaps? Is that it?

"What would you do if a Captain was critical of your flying techniques? Would you take the controls from him? Can you handle criticism?

"You had an incident at Command, went off the runway," he said as he thumbed through my log books. "What happened? Wasn't there a better way you could have handled this?" as though that journey into the woods—back then—was all my fault.

"Are you looking for big jet time and then move on? We train you and you leave, right?

"That's a lot of money out the door for all of us, if you leave. Is that why you are here?" On and on this went for a half hour. I answered each question concisely and with brevity. His speed dictating my response.

I didn't squirm and kept my composure, answering him directly and with confidence, even as he continued his interruptions. Then, abruptly it was over. He stood up, shook my hand and thanked me for my interest in People Express. "That's all," he said pointing toward the door.

"Excuse me?" I replied back, startled. "Oh, right. Okay. Thank you, too!" I said, standing up quickly. I slid my log books off his desk, turned and walked out. I was stunned. Crushed is more like it. *What the hell had happened? I blew it!* I shook my head in disgust, and now had to wait a depressing hour and a half in agony for the results.

I walked back to the employee cafeteria, sipped another cup of coffee, trying to drain away a sinking feeling. *It was totally different from this morning's politeness.* Adversarial, I thought. There was no other way to describe it, and I had trouble even coming to grips with it. Yet, I felt my replies were strong and delivered with control and directness. I never once flinched, drilling him with eye contact. There really wasn't anything I could have done better. *Sweat time, now.*

I was back at the room fifteen minutes early. It was strangely quiet, the gravity of this most important moment hanging over all of us like dark clouds. No one talked, each lost in his own convoluted inner world. I suppose we were all thinking about the good cop-bad cop grilling we had experienced. I tried reading a book, but read the same damn sentence a thousand times. My mind lost in wicked thoughts, I closed the cover, giving into futility and nervousness.

At 4:15, the door opened and the interviewers entered. They were not the cheery group we had been introduced to earlier that morning. And now there were six of them. Captain Brown spoke:

"Gentlemen, we have made our selections. And believe me, it was a very difficult decision. You are all so highly qualified. We wish we could offer each of you a position at People Express. Unfortunately, we are limited in the size of the class. If you are not selected, it is our hope that you will understand the competitive nature facing yourselves *and* us, and look upon today as a learning experience. We will be calling names in just a moment. When you hear your name, please join with one of our Captains, who will escort you down the hall. If you are not called, we request you remain seated."

The suspense only thickened the blood coursing my veins, my heart thudding and working overtime trying to move sludge to my lungs for reprieve and hope. My future was on the line. Right here. Right now. I don't know why, but a sense of foreboding was creeping up my spine. *Please God! Please don't let them call my name! Please don't!* All I could do was clutch my books, nearly denting the covers from tension playing down through my fingers.

They began calling names—alphabetically. Very slow and very methodical. Four were called. *Eleven of us left.*

"Mr. Leonard? Will you come with me please? *Oh no! Oh my God, no!* It's over, I thought, as I stood. There was no smile on the Captain's face as he nodded toward the door. We walked in slow motion down the hallway, my steps dragging like lead as though he was guiding me the "last mile." Then it came, when life finally explodes away.

"Bill, you heard what Captain Brown said, I'm so sorry," he said, placing a hand on my shoulder in comfort, directing me to the elevator. "You must realize we had to select from a highly qualified group of people, many with significantly more jet time than yourself," he said, moving his hand from my shoulder to press the down button.

"Uh, huh," I mumbled, choking back tears. What could I say? What can anyone say in defeat? What comfort can there possibly be when you are suddenly alone, facing a dismal future? It looked as though I was not meant to be an airline pilot. But the thought of flying charters for the rest of my life – I couldn't bear the thought.

I endured the awkward silence, totally crushed; it seemed like an eternity. Finally the doors opened and I hesitated a second, then shuffled in and hit the lobby button. The white light illuminated and the final flash of calamity struck deep in my brain. He turned away. I bit my cheeks in pain, trying to ward off tears welling up. Motors whirred, driving the doors toward one another. Then suddenly, a hand jutted in just before the doors shut, forcing them back open. It was the same Captain with the comforting hand.

"You know, Bill? . . . I was just thinking," he said, leaning his weight against the safety bar. "That maybe, just maybe, you'd like to come back here tomorrow—for a physical? After all, the next 737 class begins Monday. I wouldn't want you to miss it! Congratulations! Welcome on board!" He had a smile ear-to-ear, then extended his hand. I wanted to slay the bastard right then and there, but was too elated and shocked to speak. *What did he say? I'm hired!* I reached for his hand and squeezed so violently, I nearly broke it. He winced, then laughed and winked at me. "We'll call you later with the details," he said, releasing the bar. The doors whizzed past me.

"Physical is here at Newark—at the clinic," I heard his muffled words, and laughter. "And, Hey!" he shouted, behind the doors. "Have a drink on us! See you around!" His voice drowned away as the car rattled impatiently down the rails. I squeezed my eyes shut in elation.

What a fucking turn around! I was suddenly walking on water. *Where the hell is a telephone! I'm in!! Fucking A!!*

Thirty years. Thirty-years chasing an elusive dream. Finally, I've left Neverland . . . for home!

Flying the "big stuff," the powerful T-28, 1969.

With very little flight time, I was ready for carrier qualifications. On a bright sunny morning in 1969, I strapped myself into the cockpit, then took-off from Saufley Field, joining up in a formation flight, to meet the USS Wasp as it steamed across the Gulf of Mexico. I did two touch and goes and six traps on her deck that day, joining an elite group of aviators. One of the most exciting days of my life!

Instrument training. I flew in the back seat under the "bag" to simulate blind flying.

Final approach, gear and flaps down, after almost running out of fuel.

One of many attacks on the airbase at Da Nang. That night our fuel dump was hit, as well as our hanger, located near our quarters.

Back on Guam in 1971, before returning to Vietnam.

Captain William Leonardi on a Continental Airlines Boeing 727. People Express had been purchased by Continental.

I joined the training department at Continental Airlines as a Line Check Airman. Here we are on an inaugural flight into Orlando, Florida, and the introduction of Continental's new Boeing 767. I was training two Captains, each of whom were transitioning into this particular airplane. We were greeted at the terminal by the traditional spray from fire trucks.

Cindy and I, just four months after we were married. We stopped by a beautiful field for a self-timed picture. We were traveling from Pough-keepsie to Montreal.

Our family: My wife Cindy, and our daughter Lee.

IN THE MIX

I was hired that June of 1983, into Donald Burr's dreamland for aviation's future. A vision he had set in motion in 1981. Yet, behind the scenes, unknown to any of us, this charismatic man—our Chairman and Chief Executive Officer at People Express Airlines—waged a war with his ex-boss, Frank Lorenzo.

Burr had worked at Texas International Airlines (TI), which was part of Frank Lorenzo's holding company—the Texas Air Corporation. Lorenzo was a money magnet, a walking talking *dowser,* whose divining rod could attract even paper. He was an entrepreneur and corporate raider who bullied his way toward ownership of Continental Airlines. Burr had turned against Lorenzo's embroiled fight, resigning from TI, charging off to start People Express.

Frank, on the other hand, was relentless, bowling through Continental's Executive Board with unprecedented legal maneuverings. His tactics were not unlike the hostile positioning of Carl Icahn, another corporate raider whose intent was to tear through Trans World Airlines (TWA). Icahn did just that, and the company fell, slaughtered, taking everyone to their deaths, but him.

Labor unions fiercely opposed Lorenzo for his similar ruthlessness. Unfortunately, his power and money prevailed and Continental surrendered into Lorenzo's own personal empire.

By then, the battle lines had been established between these two adversaries—Lorenzo and Burr. Each played his game, knowing full well a showdown was rumbling on the horizon, like distant thunder.

Survival for either company depended upon growth and acquisition. It was their diverse management styles however, that set the tone for how this would all be accomplished.

People Express grew exponentially from 1983 until 1985, while troubles for Continental only deepened. Lorenzo's company faced mounting debt, and that, combined with churning labor unrest, slipped Continental into receivership.

It took aggressive action by Lorenzo. He submitted reorganization plans, but with questionable cost-cutting controls. Financial institutions bought into it though; so did the federal government. After many months his plans for solvency were approved, albeit with skepticism.

Continental was freed from bankruptcy and Lorenzo was off, running loose again.

In June of 1983, People Express was about to introduce the Boeing 727 to is fleet. My new hire class was to be the first to fly them, although during the hiring interview, no one mentioned that fact.

The 727 requires a three-man crew: A Captain, a First Officer, and a Second Officer—the Flight Engineer. His job is to manage all aircraft systems, to maintain aircraft log books, prepare engine performance and data cards, calculate the aircraft's weight and balance and center of gravity, advise the Captain on trim settings that are so crucial for take-off, and accomplish many other details.

Worst of all, he had to do every pre-flight and post-flight inspection, regardless of weather conditions. The Engineer was the grunt man. We called him a "plumber," the fixit man. And it looked as though I was going to be one myself.

I wore a uniform with two stripes on my sleeves, but fortunately no carpenter's bulky leather tool belt around my waist. The Engineer didn't actually fly the plane, but he was like a physician's assistant, keeping the Captain's hands sterile for delicate precise operations.

After a "walk-a-round," I always seemed to return to the cockpit with grease on my hands, or orange-colored hydraulic stains, or smears of burnt engine oil on my sparkling white shirt. I wore the pervasive odor of jet fuel like deodorant. It gave sweetness to the curious electric odor of hot electronics simmering, just below the flight deck.

During my first week of indoctrination into People Express Flight Operations, managers asked for volunteers for this new aircraft. Funny, did we really have a choice? I raised my hand anyway.

The 727 was becoming a favorite airplane with many airlines, both here in the U.S. and overseas. Unlike the smaller 737, the "Seven Two" had three jet engines in the tail. It was an extremely versatile airplane with decent range. And it was damn fast. A Mach point eight-zero machine *or better*, flying nearly nine-tenths the speed of sound. And it could carry a full complement of passengers and a fair load of cargo. The People Express planes were configured for one hundred-eighty passengers.

The 727 was one gorgeous dream machine. *Mine!* One I longed to fly ever since I saw it on the Boeing drawing boards.

As a teenager, I would drive to Kennedy or LaGuardia airports, watching in fascination as planes landed or were taking-off. I loved watching the 727 with its graceful maneuvers. It had a beautiful sweepback to its wings, and with full leading edge slats, and large trailing edge flaps (each designed to move, and increase the wings area), take-off and landing speeds were kept reasonably low for such a large airplane.

For a while I was employed as a cargo handler by Flying Tigers, at Kennedy airport, just so I could be around these fantastic machines. I had no idea that one day I would Captain one of these marvels . . . and many others, too.

But no one handed me a road map directing me toward the cockpit. Only the maze.

At every opportunity, I would venture into that surreal world of the flight deck. It was mesmerizing. Every inch of the cockpit crammed with colored lights, toggle switches, dials, levers, placards and numbers everywhere. It looked like haphazard pandemonium. Learning any of it seemed an impossible task.

But there was method in that designed madness. The forward flight instrument panels, the overhead panels, the flight engineer panel, even the throttle quadrant between the two pilots were well organized. Each carried controls for a particular system. You had to break each into sub-sections to master the confusion. *Everything has a beginning, just like life, when the senses are not necessarily friends and have not joined completely in the body's harmony.*

Much of learning means overcoming fear. Fear of what we will discover. Fear of knowing who we are. Human frailty. Yet, at one time or another we must confront it. All artists face this. After all, we *are* them. Creative people of wisdom, born to give back to *reason* that wondrous miracle of its own creation. Genius. It resides in every aspect of our humanity. And it lives in synchrony with an underlying edge of apprehension.

You see it in awkward lines slashed on blank paper by young artisans. Meanings poorly conveyed, because the strokes and messages lack understanding of principles.

It's there, throbbing in the musician as he sits alone at his keyboard, desperate for his fingers to dance, but they can't. Not yet. Because mind and muscle haven't traveled deeper into the path of theory.

You feel it in that first attempt at riding a bicycle. Tumbling, time and again, because balance does not equate with movement. But it will.

Flying too, is an art. But with its own lyric.

You have to absorb its own particular theory and balance, until every aspect settles into unconsciousness, then learns expression with Tai Chi dexterity.

The song of flight. Where each note is carefully placed in measure. And progressions develop for just one reason, then merge, softly into chords. Your finished composition.

A story told to your fingers, guiding them precisely through air. Suddenly, they are so finely tuned and alert, striking any key of essence, delicately, like a maestro. It is your masterpiece. Your opera.

That moment when you've uncovered tranquility in that elusive dimension—*time.* Where there is sensuality in *rhythm* and *timbre* even *you* can't resist. It lifts your soul so completely, letting you slide away, a hapless voyeur to your own created magic. Others witness it, too. The dazzle in their eyes as they swoon uncontrollably to your love song. Life in full meaning. The sounds of flight. The sound of dreams.

I didn't pursue flying, it was just there, bred in me. All it required was a vehicle for release and expression. The maze took care of that.

Instead of jumping into the co-pilot's seat with People Express, I was tagged to be a "side saddle manager," the lowest of the low, sitting at the engineer's panel. Getting my hands on the control wheel would have to wait a little longer.

What it really meant was that I had to take another FAA exam before 727 training began the following week in Houston.

I had taken the same test years earlier, but those scores were no longer valid. So, I did a cram review for three days, then raced to a local FAA office, composed myself, and settled in for the three-hour exam.

Timing was critical, since I'd be joining my class in Houston, but without the required certification. Even if I had completed the Engineer Ground School with Express, I still wouldn't be able to fly, not until the FAA gave me its blessing.

There were six of us at school. Each day I called home hoping for good news. I was four days into training when I received word that I had passed.

Breathing came a little easier then, as I settled into the grueling four week routine of systems and more damn testing. An uncontained immersion into engineering schematics, design philosophy, flow charts, normal and abnormal aircraft checklists, and emergency procedures. Simulators came two weeks later integrating all of it, after which, I was ready for "line flying."

When I returned to Newark, excitement buzzed through the North Terminal.

Management had just placed orders for Boeing 747s, and People Express was shifting gears for Trans-Atlantic operations. We were becoming the "big boys" on the block.

It seemed each day another new change affected us. As pilots, we were elated by these sudden twists in events. It meant more hiring and more upgrades. I'd be moving to the First Officer seat in just a couple of months, not years.

Enthusiasm flowed like electricity. You could feel it and almost see it, the energy crackling across the crew room. A charging "lets make it happen" spirit electrified all of us.

As expected, I was on the engineer panel only two months before returning to Houston for First Officer training. Express was expanding at an uncontrollable rate. But without safety valves in place, we were spending ourselves into dangerously explosive territory.

We worked hard and the traveling public caught on to our strange way of air travel: on board ticketing, choose any seat you like, pay for snacks on board, bring all the carry-on you want, fares so low you couldn't drive your car for less.

We packed the planes in hilarious panic.

For a while, people put up with our antics, amused by this wild adventure. We were like giddy teens out for a day of fun, though mesmerized by our own sudden growth. And like most adolescents, we continually misjudged our own reach because our brains couldn't adjust fast enough to our expanding bodies. We stumbled into things because we lagged dreadfully behind in maturity.

Nonetheless, the months clicked by happily for me. Less than a year after I was hired by Express, I was flying Captain on the Boeing 727. My dream suddenly a reality as I slipped off into nirvana.

None of us could see that we were growing ourselves to death.

The war between People Express and Continental was heating up. We needed to expand our route structure, but so did they.

To help our domestic feed, People Express bought two northeast commuter airlines. It was a reasonable strategy to secure a position of strength, but Don Burr wasn't satisfied. He had eyes on Denver as a mid-west hub, for expansion to the west. Naturally, so did Lorenzo. And the fight began in earnest.

Frontier Airlines, Denver, Colorado's darling child, was heading toward bankruptcy. They needed a buyer to bail them out.

Burr entered into a bidding war, fighting Lorenzo for the rights to Frontier. Guess what? Our friend Donald won! But he ultimately lost. Frontier cost People Express dearly. Far more than we had bargained for, or that Lorenzo was willing to pay.

Because of this and the other acquisitions, People Express spiraled into serious, serious debt. Adding to the mess were disgruntled employees at Frontier—our new hippie friends, or so we thought. But they resented People Express's wild management style. Our Executive Board forced them to radically alter their traditional operating practices. They looked down on us with disdain even though we had saved their lives. We were a support group for them, until their grumbling and resistance slid them backwards once again, toward bankruptcy. In the process, they took all of People Express with them.

For a few years though, leading up to that debacle, we were the rising star of the air transport industry. We could do no wrong, adding new routes and planes, arrogantly bursting onto the turf of other airlines, thumbing our noses imperiously at their shouts of anger.

Soon we were flying to Denver, Los Angeles, San Francisco, and San Diego. Even across the Atlantic, to London. We were in the big leagues now, but unfortunately, flat broke!

People Express had draped itself in flowing white gowns, like some new and imperious religious cult. Flower children bought into it, but no one else.

It didn't take other companies very long to catch on to our little secret. They began to match our fares and easily outspent us, waiting for us to falter with our huge debt and limited cash. We flamed out as expected, and found ourselves plunging in an ever-deepening spiral toward bankruptcy.

In a daring turn-around, we tried catering to "business clientele." But that soon failed.

People Express was sick. A dying experiment. We looked like weary, aged Trekkies, having gone *too long* where no man dared venture before.

The heat of competition swept east, burning toward us, over-running our home base at Newark. The turf war was now on *our* doorstep.

How do you stop a mountainous, racing fire storm? All our management could do was to stare back in disbelief. They were powerless to prevent the inevitable. People Express was in melt-down, nearly shutting its doors, strangled and out-maneuvered by larger carriers.

Lorenzo saw huge advantages in our Newark base, in our extensive equipment, and our vast route structure. Adding to that, he had money. But more importantly, he was a cunning predator, always sniffing the air, inhaling for financial weakness.

People Express was too vulnerable to withstand an attack on any front. We braced ourselves for a final assault. The airline was up for grabs, existing solely each day in an adjunct position. Who would be the victor, then tear us apart? We waited for the death blow, knowing full well who the winner would likely be.

Lorenzo was a cool player moving methodically. He positioned his Texas Air Holding company and Continental, like a master chess player. He left no option for his opponent except retreat, which we did, giving up precious territory. We were pawns, immobile. Where could we run? Lorenzo out maneuvered us at our own game. Our once precious domain falling to a new king.

Lorenzo successfully used our own business strategy against us. He bought People Express at a bargain basement price.

Soon the wiggles on the tails of our planes—the faces of people—disappeared into a defunct crowd like: Eastern, Trans World, Pan Am, North Central, Air California, Braniff, New York Air, Hughes Air West, and many others. We gave in to the "World" logo, of Continental Airlines.

We merged with them, swapping uniforms—at least for me—one last time.

It was a nasty seniority integration for us pilots. In the end, when the judge made his final ruling, I lost out. My Captaincy snatched away by the mesh of lousy numbers. Only a certain number of our Captains were allowed into the Captain ranks at Continental. And with that simple decree, came a huge loss in pay and downgrade to Second-in-Command. Even worse, under Lorenzo in 1990, Continental slipped into its second bankruptcy. But happily, Frank resigned a short time later, only to bring his malicious attack someplace else on this planet.

It took new leadership—enter Gordon Bethune—and a huge injection of funds for us to fly out of bankruptcy. The man did it. Gordon Bethune, fresh from the Boeing Aircraft Company, assumed leadership as Continental's new CEO.

Bethune developed a strong business plan with people in mind, and a simple, yet qualitative strategy for the future of the company. He turned Continental around, building it into the fourth largest airline in the United States. The fifth largest airline in the world.

My reduction in status was just another stumbling block in the maze; that is, until Bethune worked his magic. But, I used this minor setback to my advantage.

I couldn't hold a position as Captain, yet was senior enough as a First Officer to hold an international flying position. I bid and received training on the McDonald Douglas DC-10. It was some of the best flying I ever did. I loved Europe, flying to Paris, Germany, England, Scotland, Ireland, Spain, and Portugal.

That lasted two more years, until seniority numbers moved me back to where I could hold a Captain's slot, in Newark.

I jumped at the opportunity, enjoying once again command responsibility, and with it, increased salary. It's hard to describe the feeling of being in charge of a crew and passengers and your own airplane. It goes far back to that ancient mariner code of the sea, "the Captain of any vessel reigns supreme." He is law, he is executive, he is king.

And with all the changes occurring, the timing was appropriate for me to regain my Italian name—Leonardi, which I did. After six months of legal partitioning and positioning, my name change was approved by the courts, and I gained back my heritage.

Eventually I joined Continental's Flight Training Department as a "Line Check Airman."

It was that department's responsibility to ensure that the high standards set down by Bethune and his Executive Board were carried out. It was the most wonderful and satisfying position I ever held.

I continued in that capacity until my retirement in 2003. I was instrumental in many changes to our daily flight operations, our pilot flight manuals, and flight crew dispatch documents.

It seemed I became a guru for Latin American flight operations, and did more flying to South America than any other area. I flew to cities like Rio and Sao Paulo, Brazil; Bogotá, Columbia; Quito, Ecuador; Lima, Peru; and Santa Cruz, Bolivia.

Vigilance goes without saying when flying into any of these cities. Especially when crossing the enormously high and extensive spine of the Andes mountains.

SOUTH AMERICA
THE ANDES

Dancing Through The Maze

QUITO WITH JERRY

I'm alone tonight. My First Officer has less than 100 hundred hours experience in this airplane and shouldn't have been assigned to my flight, but he has been—a scheduling error. And now I must teach him all there is to know about flying to South America, and how to mingle and converse with tall sweeping mountains. Essentially, I'm on my own. When I look across at him, he looks tentative, not yet comfortable with the feel and nuances of this airplane. *It might take a year for him to gain that confidence.* Sending him down here was a mistake, he's just hanging on, not learning. So, it's just me and my machine and 185 passengers betting their flesh on safe passage, as do my seven crewmates.

Me, solo at the helm, standing watch for five-and-a-half hours babysitting, but that's my job as an instructor pilot—to teach and guide, *so quit complaining.*

Jerry is tense. So am I, as well we both should be. It will keep us vigilant. Jerry doesn't know the animal we are about to tangle with the way I do, but I know I cannot for an instant turn my back. Two other airliners—just this month—thought they could, but never returned. Vigilance will ensure our survival. Tonight we'll join with the South American continent, flying so far back in time that the Andes Mountains will seem alive, lumbering with life—which they possess—and have for millions of years, spewing volcanic ash high up into the atmosphere like a spider's web. We must avoid this ash-cloud at all costs, which waits to coat the engine blades into spinning useless metal, snaring us until we point straight down where we become dinner for Amazon beasts, and fossils for the historian. *And just how will I avoid this black cloud of ash waiting in darkness? Or the towering mountains which line our route?*

There is a glint of fear in Jerry's eyes—being shoved into some form of hell. *Bad karma, that's what his eyes tell me.* I've tried to ease his bewilderment, letting him do the take-off under my hidden sensitive fingers riding the controls.

Things will be tranquil for five hours before we descend. Jerry and I will talk and play with the computers, speak with foreign controllers, checking in with them the prescribed ten minutes before entering their airspace. Even the Cubans are friendly tonight.

I discuss the arrival into Quito.

"The runway is very short here, Jerry, don't overrun it! And stay on the glide slope, it's our life. Forget about a smooth landing too, it's meaningless if we run out of concrete. When we touch down use maximum brakes. Fry them if you have to!!"

I try not to frighten him, but there is no other way. Only realism.

The choreography to the airfield is etched on the charts before us. It is precise, bold, and not tolerant of divergence. I've reviewed it for hours and burned it into my memory, but I don't rely solely on it.

The Columbian controllers pass us off to the Ecuadorians, and this person warns us of creeping fog at Quito and low visibility, and that the tower will close in five minutes when the approach will take six, but he clears us for the arrival nonetheless.

My heart is pounding , and my veins pulsing. Once committed below the mountains . . . there is no way out! We will have to weave down valleys and over snow covered peaks—on instruments in darkness.

"Okay, Jerry. Take her down!" I order. "Approach checklist!"

We roared into Quito, Ecuador, late that night, skimming past vicious snarling mountains until the wheels slammed into a concrete runway the size of an aircraft carrier. The brakes protested and smoked and turned blazing orange, trying to seize 80 tons of runaway plane and flesh, from where it fell from grace.

Touchdown speed was insane—one hundred-ninety five-miles per hour—and decelerating ever so slowly. *One-eighty, one-seventy*. The opposite runway 'end lights' burst from the darkness, rushing toward us. We weren't slowing fast enough; yet, we were in screaming reverse with the spoilers whipped vertically into full deflection. The anti-skid pulsed wildly, using maximum energy trying to stop us. I tried to squeeze in more reverse but the interlocks said, "that's it, no more!"

Come on, Slow! Slow, damn it! One hundred-twenty, one hundred-ten. We blew by the "one-thousand foot remaining marker." *We're not going to make it!* I could see the over-run now, and the boundary fence and roadway and lights from cars. *One hundred-five, one-hundred.* The brakes clamped down like a vise, and the tires ripped along the pavement like emery cloth desperate to slow us. *Five-hundred feet. That's it! Four-hundred. THREE-HUNDRED!! Speed: Seventy . . . sixty . . . fifty.* Suddenly we're shoved forward as the plane bumps, then genuflects to a groaning halt at the north boundary. An involuntary gasp escapes my mouth. *Thank you God!* A hatch opens in my skull, a safety valve rises up, whirls alive, hissing and venting a high pressure cloud of adrenalin, apprehension, and tension into the cockpit. My body relaxed, shrinking down an inch. I took over the controls, then taxied to the gate with the wing lights blazing a trail through the eerie darkness in front of us.

You couldn't see the city, but you could smell it. The dampness sweetened with odors of food cooking on open fires. Flavors that wafted . . . just so high in the thin air, trapped in sumptuous layers that anchor in valleys of giant mountains. Yet, lingering everywhere, unmistakable reminders of nearby danger—subtle acrid fumes of sneering volcanoes.

Americano! Bienvenido a Quito!

The crew is thrilled to be here. For the next day-and-a-half it's party time. Anything that any one of them could want is within easy reach. Anything! Even the poorest tourist is a rich man in Quito.

Me? I just want to be left alone. I did my job, we're here. It's not always pretty, roughing it in the trenches and bullying down the midnight gauntlet. It never is. But we're here—wound-free and scar-less. So let me be. All I need now is my room, a hot shower, a comfortable place to hang my personal I.V., and fill it with Jose Cuervo. Drip. . . drip . . . drip. S-l-i-d-e. *S-l-i-d-e a-w-a-y.* . . .

. . . *So, what is it, Bill? What leads you here . . . to this place . . . in this time? God? The angels? karma? Or the damn maze?*

. . . *I . . . I . . . I don't know. I'm too tired. Shutdown, please! It's the mission . . . and the maze, okay? Sometimes we finish the mission young. Sometimes late. But always it gets finished! Life in full circle, okay? Who gets us where we are, and how, no one will ever know. I don't want to think about it. Leave me now. No more thoughts. Just . . . just . . . sleep. Delicious sleep . . . Bueñas Noches!*

QUITO WITH KINCAID

The beast wasn't *too* hungry last night. A rare pause for us, as we wove our way between giant mountains rising like black obelisks, teasing the approach to Quito's International Airport.

But, there was an eerie calm in the Ecuadorian darkness. As though the air were charged and energized by some mysterious vapor waiting for a spark to ignite it. And it oozed the unmistakable odor of toxic ozone. You couldn't see it, but you could taste it in your throat, and feel it burn deep in your lungs.

Yet, in this haunting stillness we performed our choreography in *relative* peace, sliding down cushioned air as soft as cotton. Gliding to a feather touchdown beneath a dome of sparkling diamonds and streaks of light from a Leonid meteor shower. The wheels kissed the concrete and eighty tons of metal and people and cargo settled gently onto the struts. We slowed, then configured the jet for a more mundane motion.

It took a few minutes for me to complete the logbook entries, then positioned a sequence of switches that shunted electricity from ship's power back to ground power. I sat a moment with troubled thoughts gnawing at me. Captain Tom Kincaid's performance left me with serious doubts about his ability. Throughout the flight he seemed uncertain about international procedures. This was a "route check" for him and a "South American" qualification. It was a "show me what you've got flight!" But Kincaid's actions flowed like water looking for an easier path. His preparation for such a demanding flight was poor, and he asked way too many obvious questions. The answers were right there on his charts. Every pilot I've ever flown with knows this. They are the abc's of flying. But not for Kincaid. He had a thirst to be shown things. Even menial things.

Our arrival into Quito this evening under starry skies was not routine. It rarely is. Had I not been there with Tom, our flight might have turned into tragedy. Our computers and moving map displays failed at the worst possible moment as we descended down the thirty mile long valley. Captain Kincaid became pre-occupied, almost obsessed with rebooting them. I waited as long as I dared. The plane became an out-of-control missile closing on the mountains at over 360 feet per second. Little time if any to avoid disaster. I gave him a second longer to act; when he didn't, I yelled at him, "SWITCH TO MANUAL! TURN HARD RIGHT—THIRTY DEGREES! GET US BACK ON COURSE INTO THE VALLEY! HOLD YOUR ALTITUDE! "Hey, man!" I said, glaring at him. "You lose situation awareness here and you're dead, *as in it's all over! Capish!* There *is* no room for error. Use everything you've got. You have to know your position every second. American Airlines lost it one night, at Cali, Columbia, slamming into a ridge line because they weren't sure where they were! The airways here are narrow with mountains all over the place. It's imperative that you do not deviate far off course, or you're dead. And so is everyone else!" I waited for his reply, or any sign that he understood the gravity of his mistake. But he merely shrugged his shoulders as if too say, "Oh, well, we're not in Cali." I was dumbstruck! I don't know what world he was living in, but it sure wasn't mine! How he ever got this far was beyond me. He offered no insight into his thinking or logic. All I could do now was to guide him through the remainder of the approach. It was just one more thing he did that made me seethe. I had given him chance-after-chance to prove himself, not only to me, but *to himself.* He failed in every instance.

I was the last off the plane, walking quietly toward the hotel van, lost in thought. Not one of the crew or the passengers will ever know how close to death they had come. And now Captain Kincaid seemed cheerful to be here, as though nothing alarming had occurred. The twenty minute ride to the hotel was an ordeal for me. Kincaid's very presence revolted me. *I never want to sit this close to him again. Right! But it's the job! Tomorrow I'll hand the bastard the bad news.*

My room was spacious. The Captain's suite. I loved it. A steaming shower is what I needed now, most of all. And a liter of red wine and a cup of tannic acid. *I need to calm down.* I stripped quickly, then stood under the hot spray for a full fifteen minutes. It was soothing. The heat flushing my face and neck cherry red. And the heavy volume of water massaged away the tension in my back with all the strength of a masseuse. I dried off and dressed in workout clothes, enjoying the beauty of this immense room and the stillness of the night. The crew would be off to the bars to party and then to who-knows-where. They are supposed to let me know where they will be, but they never do. And I could care less. They come here for fun, for the ease of things and the dollar's value. I can only hope they don't prey upon the kindness and gentle naiveté of these hardworking people. I walked over to the picture window looking out at the mountains.

Dots of light from small homes danced erratically up toward the night sky. Living here and farming so high up always amazed me. Terracing was the ancient solution for such difficult survival. I watched slow moving cars and buses and trucks serpentine up the steep roadway, their engines straining against the tug of a three-mile high incline. They looked like faint pin pricks of light moving like faraway stars.

One a.m., and I still had more paperwork to do, and deal with, Kincaid. My decision had been made back in the cockpit, even though the second half of our trip still lay in front of us. I thought about the advice a fellow training Captain had offered me when he was confronted by a similar situation. "If there is a doubt about someone's ability, *then there is no doubt!*" That simple message only reinforced what I already knew to be true. I opened my flight case, yanked out the proper documents and moved over to the desk. I completed the "Line Check form" as . . . unsatisfactory. I could never let Tom fly down here again! Not alone! Not in the darkness! Not ever! I wrote my evaluation and recommendations, then signed my name. Unfortunately for Kincaid, his flying career was now in serious jeopardy. But that was his problem, not mine. I clicked off the lights, rolled into bed, anxious for a peaceful night's sleep. Tomorrow I would go to one of the outdoor cafes on Amazonas Avenue. Sip coffee in the cool morning air, write, and watch beautiful women. In the afternoon I'll trade "black gold" for wine, and do more of the same.

The sun blazed into my room all too soon, flicking cobalt blue twilight back into the confetti darkness of a top hat. I gave in, easing myself out of bed. There was much I wanted from this day.

Ohh . . . but the shower felt good. Sending a thousand pleasing fingers to massage away my fatigue. They caressed and warmed then teased, until every cell woke so that I would know I was in a maddening race with the sun—again. Me, selfish and greedy because of the Earth's damn fast spin. It should slow. But it never would, so I did, pausing a moment, trying to snare skewed thoughts that blew everywhere across my brain:

We are so delicate aren't we? Trying to survive on this fragile planet of ours. Never comprehending that the only real mortal enemy to life . . . is time. Something that can't be packaged, worn, sipped, or absorbed. It seems I've been racing the hours and years, ever since my Mother and Father nodded to fire burning in their eyes. There is so much I want. So much to have. It is all out there waiting. For everyone. Whether it is here, or at home. Or up there for me, riding the wind. Wings were inevitable extensions of my mind. My karma, my incarnation without choice. How tedious life would be without challenge. Without imagination, and thirst for creativity. I'm gone, for the journey.

I dressed quickly and raced to meet the day.

110

A wind eddied off the mountains gliding into this deeply notched valley. It overran the capital, tunneling between tiny concrete homes, tall apartment buildings, hotels, and narrow side streets. It funneled along Amazonas Avenue where I walked, burning into my face like an astringent. The odors it carried were puzzling. A cauldron of foods cooking on open fires, smells of ash from Pichincha volcano four miles west, motor exhaust, even a faint trace of ozone. Everything but the flavor of landscape and flowers to ease away foreign tastes lingering on my tongue, and strange aromas wafting beneath my nose. *But the mountains are so green. Where is the smell of grass and trees and the loam of the soil?* I couldn't place any of this, not against the hills I knew back home with their own telltale fragrances. Everything here was different, as to be expected. After all, I was just a visitor, and this *is* Ecuadorian air. It runs free with its own emblematic flavor and embellishment. These people have endowed rights to all of it.

With the wind came a chill, though I knew it would warm later, when the sun finished its climb and the Earth spun a little further. Already the rays struck with a vengeance, piercing without opposition through the thin atmosphere. The warmth felt good, offsetting the cold—at least for now, bringing a glow to my face, and the first alarm of impending sunburn to my brow.

The Valdez brothers must have known I would be here on Amazonas this morning, sending a personal gift of their finest black gold here. I savored the essence of this rich blend, at ease with myself, sitting at my favorite outdoor cafe with a spectacular view of the mountains. The same mountains I sped by late last night. There was a semblance of peace buried here in the early morning confusion, even as the city came to life, though I had to ignore many peddlers who waved their goods at me for quick sales. Some of them I couldn't.

A young boy approached. He couldn't have been older than five or six. His hands filthy black, his short sleeved shirt frayed, threads flying like malnourished flags from his sleeves. His legs must have been freezing since he wore only shorts. And his thin ankles were as dirty as his hands. The shoe box he carried seemed too large for his frail body.

"Señor? You like shine?" he asked with a suspicious gleam in his eyes.

"No, niño, gracias. Tengo sandalias," I said, in my attempt at Spanish. He looked at me surprised, then down at my sandals. "I shine toes, tambien?" he answered back, hope gleaming in his eyes. I smiled, saying again, "No niño. Gracias. Pero aquí," and gave him a shiny, Susan B. Anthony dollar. He examined the coin with a deep scowl across his tan face. "Gracias, Señor" he said. But it seemed more of a question than a sincere thanks.

"Niño, momento? Dondé esta su mama?" I asked. "No se!" he replied in a tired dry voice. He turned as he spoke, walking toward the next table of hope, flipping my coin as though trying to measure its worth. I looked up and down the street as far as I could see for his mother, or his father. There were no anxious stares following after him.

. . . What have I done? Did I bring him any closer toward a dream. Does he have one? Have I just prolonged his time in the maze? Is there an exit for him . . . to climb through? Am I a victim only to be smirked at when he rounds the corner? Will my dollar find him an education? I shook my head, angry with myself because I should have done more, and that only brought back unpleasant thoughts to Captain Kincaid. A man with everything, yet nothing. *Such a fool! Jeopardizing a career because of laziness. They should trade places, Kincaid and the boy. Maybe he'd get it then.* He seems to have no idea that flying here is not to be taken lightly. I wiped away my angry feelings, whisking them aside to the issue and irritation file wilting deep in my brain. I sipped more coffee, read a little, even wrote between introspective looks at the tall peaks I conquered yesterday. Not with a mountain climber's ax and pitons, but with an invention that simply shot me up there higher, and light years faster.

Amazonas was crowded with people now. School children in blue and black checkered uniforms, laughing, walking in groups. *My little friend should be with them, but he isn't.* There were some well-dressed men and women in corporate wardrobe, too. Quito's elite minority. And there were farmers down from the mountains, knitting hats and sweaters and shawls, preparing for the weekend market by the hotels. *West meets West, and the world implodes.*

It was a reprieve to be sitting alone, even though I had to think about the crew and tomorrow's flight. I had no idea where they were. *Probably not checking in to stall any chance of us repositioning the airplane, should it be necessary. They are smart.* It would take me hours to find them. *Not my problem.* I finished my coffee, walked down the street for my Spanish lesson, deciding that later on I'd explore, then return to the café for afternoon wine and . . .? But the hours compressed, speeding west beyond my grasp.

Where has the day gone? All too soon the sun turned orange, falling deep into the mountains. The sky slowly lost its vibrant blue color, turning deep grey, and a feeling of melancholy swept over me. It had been a pleasant day, but reality and hazards of tomorrow crept back in. I wrote a little more, quickly in fact, in the fading light, then reluctantly got up and ambled back to the hotel. Another restless night was on the way.

The view from the Captain's suite at the Marriott was impressive. Lush green mountains rose not far from the hotel — a mile or less. We sit anchored here, 9000 feet above sea level, but these towering volcanic giants leap another 8000 feet up from the valley floor. They stand imperious, like glorified chess warriors on guard to protect us. There are times, though, when they become rattled and disturbed, then renege on a mission to serve the good of the people, turning against them, striking down with vengeance that slays and destroys.

These are not the sheer peaks of the massive Himalayas, or the needle summits of the Pyrenees. Not here at least. Such snow-covered mountains lie a short distance from Quito's center. Come daylight we will have to weave ourselves between them, trying desperately to out-climb their incredible heights, as we turn East for Columbia. I looked away from the window for a second, back at the night table alarm clock. *Three a.m.* In four hours the challenge would begin. But I'm ready.

It's quiet here in my room and I'm enjoying the comfort and warmth, having slowly adjusted to Quito's high altitude with its less oxygen. Outside, there's not a whisper of a breeze. The flowers are wrapped tight, resting, and the heavy frond leaves droop undisturbed. They sleep, as I should be doing, waiting patiently for the sun's magic to wake them. The dim light from the clock reflects in the glass and imprints against the mountains. I can see in and I can see out, all at the same time. A strange illusion projecting like a mirage. *Deception in reality.* My thoughts slow, relaxing a moment as they wander deeper into that ether of nowhere:

I want to be home. To my family. To my friends. To that meaningful world according to Leonardi. To ride back home at light speed to my space. To that place where I find belonging, rather than endure six grueling hours at snail's pace, plowing north through the atmosphere. I invoke the Trinity, asking its support. Pitting each of Them against this insane sculpture only They could have created: Nature and us. I have no control or rights in Their spiritual world, and even less out there with nature. So where does that leave me? A lone companion in the company of Supremacy that appears, I will never understand. Not with these senses. Which only adds to my confusion. It seems all I'm left with is awe, respect, and humility, and endless wandering. To marvel from a distance at a power so great, raining down life force over this incredible tiny world. This Blue Dot we call Earth. Is that it? I wonder?

I looked higher into the night sky. And there, hovering in that black sea was Jupiter, etched against white tendrils of the Milky Way. His light streaming down as though a code. I pressed my face against the cold glass looking even higher.

Jupiter-Zeus. One and the same. December's Master . . . If you are a believer. I suppose I am, though with caution. But what part of the Trinity is He? The Religious? The Myth? The Celestial? I waited for a reply, but Jupiter ignores such trivial questions from mortals. He remained silent and pragmatic.

Jupiter. Lord of ancient Gods, tossing energy and power down at me-the Ninth Sign of the Zodiac—shooting his energy across the ecliptic southwest, lighting it. Then piercing into my home — Sagittarius, infusing life into The Archer and Centaur. Man-Beast. *Am I the thread of such paradox?* But, there always seems to be an uneasiness lurking within me.

Sometimes, I am the Hunter. Other times the Beast. Sometimes I draw back on the string, straining the bow. Other times, I am the arc and the arrow. Sometimes I tear the skies, hungry to explore. Other times, I dive insane and kill the freshness I've uncovered. Is this madness like that of a Minotaur? Or is it his rage that I suffer?

Crazy, wild thoughts! I had to shake my head in disbelief as though they can't be mine. "Bill? You *really* do need some rest!" So I turn from the window and move to the bed. Late night ushered in, then disappeared like vapor.

I'm tossing as usual. Sleep never comes easy for me here. Not when I'm facing two dangerous take-offs into the rugged spine of the Andes mountains. *At least this morning I'll see them coming.* I know I can't count on Captain Kincaid for help, but then again, would I really trust him anyway? So I'm alone, which is fine by me. Instructing can be a lonely endeavor. I looked down the short hallway adjacent to my bed, toward the entry door. There were no envelopes or messages slipped silently beneath, nor were there any red flashes on my phone from stored messages. I assumed the Newark crew had arrived safely and that there were no serious issues with our plane. I used another hour reviewing my departure procedures, emergencies, and alternates, as well as the arrival and departure plates for Bogata. Once we're strapped into the cockpit, time would compress and there would be little chance to give these charts the intense study they require. Safety was written boldly into those pages. I read and absorbed until I couldn't take it any longer. Sleep came, but in restless waves, as my mind would wake to another question that needed answer. Up, down, a repetition I performed all night long. I slept procedures, and dreamed the choreography my machine and I would have to perform as we raced concrete, greedy for cushioned air. But I didn't care, people were safe with me. And come dawn . . . I was heading home.

ALMOST HOME

President Gutierrez is sipping scotch in First Class—he can't help. Neither can any of his aides, nor the other hundred innocent passengers already ashen-faced by our prolonged weather delay.

"Continental 1866, Quito tower? Do you have El Presidente de Ecuador on board?"

"Yes, Quito. We do," I reply. *How can I lie when a small army of Red Coat troops block the nose of my airplane? Rows of them standing at attention, rigid like the Terra-Cotta soldiers of Xiang, China. Can't you see them? Only they are not Chinese, my friend. They dress like British warriors whisked suddenly from a forgotten century into the future. Ripped from painful dark years in American history, dropped here. Brilliant red targets comically obvious by modern warfare standards.*

"Weather North remains below three-hundred meters and visibility one kilometer," he continues. "Will you depart?"

"No, Sir. We require ceiling above two hundred meters, and visibility at or better than three kilometers."

He pauses a moment. "Are you able to depart, south?"

"No, Sir. We still require three kilometers visibility!" He's quiet again. Seconds pass, then, "Continental 1866, Quito tower?

"Go ahead, Sir," I reply.

"Visibility South is now *three* kilometers. Will you accept Departure Number Eight—Kolta?"

What! I look out my side window but can barely make out the bases of the mountains. All I see are fingers of mist and heavy fog sliding toward us, snatching away the runway. *Will I accept departure number eight?*

"Quito? Continental 1866, repeat the visibility, please."

"Quito visibility South is three kilometers."

It must be Gutierrez visibility. I squint in desperation trying to locate that mysterious black hole the controller is looking into. We're all tired by this three hour ordeal; even I'm getting edgy. We still have to deal with the immensely dangerous departure from Bogotá, yet here we sit, a decorative ornament at Mariscal Airport in Ecuador.

If he says the visibility is three kilometers, then so be it. His report satisfies all legalities, transferring the difficult Go-No Go decision, back to me. But, will he ensure that we won't strike rock instead of cloud as we rip air into atoms, or that the engines won't glaze and falter, swallowing tons of ash from spewing Cotopaxi and Sincholagua volcanoes? Certainly, I can accept the departure. How confident are you—Captain?

"Okay, Quito. Continental 1866 will depart runway seventeen, and fly Departure Number Eight. Permission to start." Kincaid looks at me quizzically—*are you sure about this, Captain?*

I glance at him. It's not that he says this, but I can see a hint of fear glistening on his palms, and beads of moisture highlighting his eyes like glitter. A harrow must have cut into his brow, leaving deep lines of worry. *Kincaid farmed in another life. Yes. I'm certain.*

"We fly dead on the Sid, (Standard Instrument Departure), we'll be okay," I say, assuring him. *I have doubts too, but why tell him? We both know the risks.*

"There is more maneuvering room to the South," I add. "Reports place the ash just west of us." I hand him an alert from the weather service buried deep in a mound of papers.

"We'll be in a left turn almost immediately after take-off and heading north." He nods his head, understanding, though not completely agreeing.

"Continental, 1866, you are cleared to start. New clearance when ready."

"Go ahead," Kincaid acknowledges.

"Clearance remains the same except: Departure Number Eight—Kolta, Upper Amber five-five-zero, Bogotá. Maintain flight level three-three-zero." Kincaid reads back the clearance while I reprogram the computers for the new runway, the new SID, and the southern "Special Engine Out Departure Procedure." It is a very complex pattern that must be flown precisely, especially when friendly air can turn solid at any second.

We taxi toward the runway, the tires thump grudgingly on flat spots from sitting overnight, the plane ladened down with fuel. *They'll round out shortly.*

"Quito, tower? Continental 1866 is ready."

"Continental 1866: Line up and wait!" the controller orders.

I ease the Boeing into position. Light rain trickles down the windscreen, I can't see more than 600 feet down the two-mile long runway. *I have to believe there is a pathway beyond.* Make it so, I pray.

"Wipers on, when cleared for take-off," I tell Kincaid. "Off—with gear up!"

"Right," he replies.

We sit, and we wait. Poised. The tension builds. Adrenalin flows. Vibrations strafe up and down the fuselage in waves. *What's the delay now?* My legs pulse uncontrollably pressing down on the brakes, trying to hold back 80 tons of eager metal and flesh. *Are they clearing airspace for El Presidente? Of course! Right. He reigns! But?... All the King's horses and all the King's men cannot. Cannot... what, Captain? Defy the maze? No one can. Nothing can.*

Idle, meaningless thoughts while we sit.

... It doesn't matter. I love these moments. The excitement. Me with my machine. She is so beautiful. She lives and I'm an anxious awestruck lover. I'm ready to dance. Let me take you away ... to my world. To serenity. To a place of unimaginable splendor and astonishing power. It beckons. Don't wait! Don't waste ...

"Continental 1866, cleared for take-off."

"Roger," I hear Kincaid reply to the tower, and a distant click as he turns on the wiper switch.

I hold the brakes even harder while pushing up the throttles, checking and double checking each engine instrument for the slightest hesitation, or missed beat. There is none. The entire plane bucks and lurches like a chained ferocious cat. I push the power levers forward to the stops, easing off the brakes at the same time. Restraints explode off the cat's neck. She bolts, sprinting for freedom. *Run, love. Run. . . Away!*

I tease the rudder pedals nailing us bull's eye down the centerline. But almost as soon as we move we are swallowed by dense fog, catapulting us into a diffuse world of white angels. It is as though we don't exist. Never have existed.

"Damn!" The wipers are hellaciously loud. I can hardly concentrate. The tires rumble, unable to find rhythm, changing beat each half-second, whistling against grooved concrete. They drone, whine in protest, buzz a high pitch vibrato as we near take-off speed. *It's taking forever. I'm having trouble homing on the dim white flashes racing beneath the nose. The crescendo is close. I can sense it. It's beyond belief.*

Kincaid calls, "One-hundred."

"Roger!" I acknowledge, checking that both my airspeed gauges agree with his.

Seconds later he calls, "V-One."

. . . No stopping now. Life is forward, not back. Each of us alone with destiny. I'm alone fighting through the maze.

I take my right hand from the throttles and caress the control yoke . . . *The seduction begins.*

"Rotate!" Kincaid shouts.

I ease back on the stick. *My hands gently coax her.* The nose rises. The tires spin insane. *This is it, my love. Come with me.* We point fifteen-degrees toward heaven. *Nirvana exists. My heart is pounding from the thrill. From danger and pleasure being so intensely joined to her. Savage power and fear churning deep within me as I embrace her tenderly.* A second later the main tires rip away from Earth.

"Gear. Up," I call.

"Center autopilot. On."

"LNAV (lateral-computer generated mapping). On." The plane glues itself to the computer-generated outbound track. We rocket through 14000 feet in a heartbeat, retracting the flaps only then, so we can accelerate and blur metal!

. . . We are clean and we are free. And she is mine to possess now. I tease her. Roll her. Expose her. Devour her sensuality. Ravage her until she loves me back even more wildly, punishing me into total ecstasy. She gives, then gives even more, and I take like a greedy child. She is power in the Sun. I sink to animalism. Helpless. Nothing has more meaning than our touches. Our grace. The horizon fades into rolling plains. Everything turns grey. We are locked . . . two of us alone, against life.

. . .I live for you! I am your protector. God. I have found reason.

Dancing Through The Maze

THE ARRIVAL

Bogotá was not the demon my fatigued mind conjured late last night. We arrived here at Eldorado airport, Columbia, punching through fog, touching down in a plume of white spray and blue smoke. It was as though an illusionist, in his moment of triumph, whirled and pranced across an immense stage, gracing and imitating the eloquent art of Tai Chi Chuan. Suddenly he stops, focusing intently off into the distance, a devious smile adding to the moist gleam in his eyes. Slowly and dramatically, he lifts his arms high above his head, then snaps open his hands in a final heart-stopping crescendo. Bolts of lightning burst from his fingers. In that startling flash and thunderous clap, we appear. A giant raptor, wings spread wide, talons exposed, poised for attack. But we flutter instead, touching gently to earth. Not to devour. And not to terrorize. Arriving mysteriously from one time warp into another. Again.

I taxied slowly down a long ribbon of concrete, watching closely for our ramp entrance, maneuvering carefully so as not to strike a wing tip, which I can never see. *I do believe we have wings, though they remain totally beyond sight.* Even craning my neck and pressing my face against the side window, I still can't see them, or the engines. *I know that they are there because we are here. I'm a believer.* I eased to a stop in sequence with the lineman, just as he crosses his arms. I set the brakes; move the start levers to cut-off, shutting the engines down. Off to my left I see the same man raise orange-lighted wands to shoulder height, then arc them down toward his thighs, touching the ends together. Chocks are in place, is his signal. As soon as I see this, I release the parking brake handle, giving the eight main wheels with their massive carbon discs, as much air circulation as possible to dissipate heat. *They have got to cool. Must cool, before we attempt another takeoff. Hot brakes would never halt our galloping momentum as we compete down the runway, rushing to compress air. No. Not a single joule of energy remaining in those sizzling glowing pads if we needed them. Not for a panic stop. Thank you God of Water, for cool spray to the wheels. One less worry to contend with.* Still I was very careful taxiing, using reverse thrust to slow our pace, minimizing any friction on the brakes. Not an authorized procedure, since the engines are really vacuum cleaners gone berserk, anchored securely inside an asylum. They suck in anything in their way: air, dirt, nuts and bolts, even people. The ground director must stand at least fifty-feet away, and not in a direct line with the engines during start or shut-down. That is, if he values tomorrow. I call for the "Parking Checklist." Kincaid reads from the plastic card, and I touch and call out each lever, switch, and knob. He nods his head to each of my replies, then says, "Parking Check is complete."

For a precious few seconds I relax. Inhale long and deep, preparing for the next wave of mind-crunching decisions. I'm excited, nonetheless, knowing there is just one more takeoff and landing. Then I'm home. *Home.* Where I can water the roots of my sanity. *Distort away those tense hours ripping air at wicked speed, blurring every second of them into oblivion with multiple glasses of soothing red wine. . . . Yeah.*

Beyond the forward window I see a dark cloud of anger in the gate area. I can almost hear the screams and curses, taste the acid words of frustration. The walls offer little protection. They bulge with rage like bursts from a runaway bellows.

Vacations planned months in advance, are ruined. Business ventures set in dollars, scrubbed. Weddings postponed. Reunions delayed. The only thing not touched is death. It doesn't care, even laughs, mocking the pandemonium. What are a few more hours measured against eternity?

I shake my head. Safety is not the issue here, though it should be. *I think El Presidente would like to stand me up against a wall, even though he invited me to join his political cabinet. So too, agree the passengers.*

Yet, inside, the crust of society has turned malicious—doctors, lawyers, teachers, philosophers, even psychologists. I see it playing like a movie, only projected on glass. Killing might be on their minds. If I tell them they still stand vertical without support, moving gaily under their own power, would it make a difference?

I know where I have to be, and cannot possibly do exclusive work imbedded in Mother Earth. Señors y señoras, shovels will not be necessary to scrape you up and deliver you to your destinations. You are safe with me. Comprendé? But blame has to be directed somewhere. Certainly not on the weather. *Señor, we will leave shortly. Patience, por favor. Have fun, say hello to the President of Ecuador. I'm much too busy right now, to speak. Relax, Señor.*

None of this works because it is all about self. Regardless of circumstances. The self needs to be where anxiousness says it should be. Even if it has to drill its own body through stone to get there. Logic ceases to exist. And how all this will be accomplished is of little concern. Jam every crazed passenger into this aluminum tube and they are suddenly happy, even rational. *And you, Captain. You must deliver these ranting souls to a place not far from nirvana. On with you.*

I scribble entries into the log book as fast as I can, but the main cabin door thuds open before I complete the engine data. In seconds there will be an onslaught of agents forcing their way into the cockpit, thrusting a mound of papers at me that normally would take me twenty minutes to analyze, yet in reality, all I'll have is five. They will welcome us with smiling faces, yet sneer, pressuring us to turn this plane quickly, questioning me about the number of passengers I can take and the weight of cargo we can board. They would like my answers to echo their desperate hope for speed, to usher us away fast. What they urgently need is freedom. To re-invent themselves and run as far as possible from insanity buzzing in the gate area. To fill the vacuum of our rapid departure with a burst of perfume and refreshing cool air. "Come again in another lifetime," is the veiled smile sweeping their harried faces. "Say goodbye to Bogotá, Captain. Hasta luego."

But they will never understand the worry pressing me deep into my seat. All they see are papers as they wait impatiently for my fuel order, holding their breath for my treasured signature on the Captain's release form. Signing it says, I have analyzed every minute detail and agree the flight can depart safely. All problems henceforth are mine. And once away from the gate, the federal government will come looking for me, or my family, but not the agents if I crash and burn.

What they will never see written on those pages, but seared in my mind are the risks we face leaving Bogotá:

Will the tires hold together at two-hundred twenty knots when they are only rated to two-fifteen? Have the brakes cooled sufficiently for takeoff, or do we risk a blowout from high temperatures if they haven't? Will the air temperature stay at fifteen degrees Celsius, or rise even a single degree, thinning the air so we become too heavy for the engines to accelerate us in the confines of the runway? Can we clear the mountains at our takeoff weight? What if we lose an engine? Have I memorized the escape procedure? Do I have the fuel needed to make it to Newark, and then to my alternates if need be? Is there maneuvering fuel boarded for thunderstorm avoidance and holding delays? Will Newark's weather permit a low approach? Will our alternate remain suitable for use should we execute a 'go around'? But we are Category Three, even if Newark is only allowing landings down to Category Two. I can still do it. To hell with them! I'll shoot an auto land and let the plane land itself if I have to. But I may still have to leave behind some cargo or people or both. I need the extra gas. They always short change me here on

126

fuel. Wait and see, Captain. You'll know shortly.

I try to accommodate, but in the end it doesn't matter. It is *I* who wield the power. My decision, and only mine. One way or another. *So Señor, be very careful what you say. I have angels watching over me.*

As the cockpit door opens, I turn in my seat to face them. They bring the odor of anguish with them. I smell passenger rage and disgust smeared on their clothing, percolating up like vapor. Invisible angry passenger aromas wafting off wrinkled jackets and stained white shirts, sullying the warm electric odor of my home, here in the cockpit.

Tread lightly in my domain, Señors. You never know where lightning may strike.

They thrust the flight plan and piles of paper at me. "Good afternoon, Captain." And so the rush begins.

Dancing Through The Maze

NORTHBOUND

The departure from Bogotá was uneventful, that is, until two hours into the flight, when that vague image of the Grim Reaper began to materialize.

We're dead. I've killed every one of us. My passengers. My crew. Me. Right, even me. But do I really count in God's eyes, since I'm the executioner, the murderer?

"Anything from Havana, yet?"

Kincaid looks at me through feminine eyes. They sparkle with innocence yet harbor chameleon agenda. What attachment they share with his mind, I can't read. Capricious and transient is all I can think, while I search for recognition in their childish movement. *He seems oblivious, bored and hungry, asking again when lunch will arrive. He doesn't feel the early signs of fear positioning for assault on us. If he did he would squirm a little, sharing the cold wriggling up my spine, sneaking stealthfully into my brain.* "Why do you ask, Captain?" his delicate expression seems to convey.

Why? Why do I ask you, Captain Kincaid . . . about Cuba? Because in ten minutes we may be feasting on missile, rather than lobster. Shellfish not drenched in butter but harshly seasoned in metallica, then seared in flame for effect. Our lunch, you irresponsible shit, unless you get us a clearance across Fidel Land. We don't have fuel to circumvent this island sand castle that steals essence from its people, and drains life from the sun like a sycophant. Are you getting any of this, Kincaid?

"Well, stay on it," I say, in disgust. "We are closing on the Cuban Air Defense Information Zone (ADIZ). If you don't get through in the next minute, switch to secondary, and give the position report. Keep giving it." *Maybe Kincaid is unaware the Cubans shot down two planes last year for violating their borders. I doubt it. But am I sitting next to a Captain? God, I wonder? I don't want to be the first commercial airliner to splinter across this island of illusion.* I shake my head in bewilderment at his lack of concern.

"Right. Okay," he says, slowly picking up his microphone with one hand, switching frequencies with the other. I watch him a second longer just to be sure, then resume my own communications with Jamaica Control. I tell them we are unable to "read" Havana, can they pass our position to them, and also our estimate for the coastal ADIZ? I pause a moment for their reply. I hear them talking, but not to me. *One more second, I'll give them.* "Kingston, do you read Continental 1866, with my request? . . . Kingston, Continental 1866? Do you read? Over?" I'm getting frantic now. No one talks to us and we are still not cleared through Cuban airspace. I'm running out of options.

. . . No. The Cuban's wouldn't dare shoot at us. Or would they? But we have the over-flight permit, our Holy Grail, so they know our itinerary. We paid dearly for it in greenbacks. But Captain, the charts are explicit: All aircraft entering Cuban airspace must maintain two-way radio contact, at least ten minutes prior to border crossing. Aircraft that do not will be intercepted or shot down.

So what is it Captain? Cross, or turn away? Turn and run and land where? Montego Bay, or back to Bogotá*? There's always Baranquilla, or Cartegena. Call the company, let them know the situation? No! No time left. Cross or leave now, it's too late. What will it be? . . .*

I ease the throttles forward slightly, then adjust our track two degrees north. Kincaid looks at me with dead eyes floating helpless in a roiling grey sea. "Switch to emergency frequency and give our position, don't stop until I tell you." He nods and shrinks down in his seat.

President Gutierrez doesn't realize he is raising his final sip of wine to his lips. But I do. The woman in 24-C feels the first nudge of her growing child inside, it is her last moment in euphoria. I am so sorry for you both. And the two lovers flushed with passion hiding beneath blankets toward the rear, fail one breath short of nirvana. I chose wrong, my friends. And the other one hundred ninety passengers and crew, they too ride with me through the maze. Each and every one a representative of this planet Earth. People of wealth, people of poverty, people of faith, people fighting tendrils of death. I am their Moses, but lead them astray now. I've led my own life astray . . .as did Moses at the Burning Bush. And God didn't catch it. But, judge me. Judge him. Judge us all gathered here... We are consecrated for better or worse. All of them married to me, looking for bliss.

We punch through the ADIZ entering that elastic dimension of fear. It blows backward across the cockpit like a bow wave of dread. Nothing tangible. Nothing visible. Yet it constricts reason and soils the air here on the flight deck. The passengers are immune because this is my sin. Not theirs. It glues me to my seat so I will never ever forget violation. I wait for punishment. I even start the timer. *Fifteen minutes.* If we're lucky, if we cheat undetected, we'll see the sixteenth through Miami's eyes. Kincaid is finally getting the point and I watch him sweating profusely. Our last try—relaying through other aircraft—has already failed, so there is not much more to do. We are over land now, rocketing across hell, waiting for the God of death—Thanatos—to strike. I sit back, bracing, even as I dial in the "lost communication code." In thirty years of flying I have never used this emergency option. I do now as a last resort. Maybe . . . just maybe, the Cubans will see it and understand, laugh a little, but let me squirm free to Miami. I set numbers into the transponder, 7-6-0-0. It says to all radar operators of any country that we have lost our ability to use our radios, that we are proceeding as initially cleared from our departure point, *on filed course,* and at *present altitude.* So be it.

    . . .Seven-hundred seconds to life and freedom. It's maddening. Click . . .Click . . .Click. . .

Dancing Through The Maze

CUBA

Too late, we're already inside the ADIZ and I have to eat fear. Not the same kind I felt climbing away from Da Nang, racing up through the night toward Hanoi. I was stealth then, and a target playing against the odds. Accepted fear . . . without choice.

I don't know Raul Castro, or his air force. But I do know he has Mikoyan Gurevich (MiG)-23's, and 29's, and they do sting, thanks to Comrade Russia. "Brothers to the Rescue" found that out as they approached Havana in 1996. Two unarmed Cessnas from Miami vaporized by Cuban missiles. Four men and metal debris falling piecemeal like feathers into the sea. Not a single chance at defense.

Now I'm sneaking inland like they did, swallowing on that sour taste of self-generated bile, sitting alert from an electric punch of adrenalin. Garnishes lavishing fear. So avoidable . . . If only I had turned around . . . .

Will the attack be frontal? Or come out of the sun? Or from my six o'clock? Does it really matter? It didn't for Korean Airlines flight 007, Captain. The Russians summarily executed two-hundred sixty-nine people for straying across Sakhalin Island, sacred Russian territory. And for each of those people there was no trial by jury, or court appeals drawn out for years. None. They were raped. Taken from innocence with not a moment of farewell. No embraces. No tear-filled kisses. Not one last chance to say . . . I love you so . . . you have given meaning to my life.

The next twenty minutes were the most anxious moments in my life. *Would Fidel and Raul be generous this afternoon—even smart - realizing their gold depositories would continue to grow if they would only ignore the hate throbbing down their edgy trigger fingers?*

We're halfway across, now. I can still hear communications from Cubana, and American, and British West Indies, and Delta, and many other airliners talking to Havana. Everyone but us. There is no indication of an impending threat to our aircraft.

We close rapidly on Cuba's North shore. Uncertainty remains and it is nerve wracking. We are running the gauntlet. I hold the over flight permit against the sweat in my palms, our ticket out of hell. I read it again, several times in fact. It is accurate. Issued for my flight today, with a specific code authorizing the crossing. When I look down at my charts, the bold warnings are still emblazoned there. *Fidel would be a fool to risk an international incident and shoot at us, downing a civilian airliner. So Captain? Are these warnings simply a bluff?* I sit ill-at-ease, staring at the permit which almost dissolves into a sticky pulp. *I'm sweating like never before.* And yet, each passing minute is another mile closer to safety as we race for North shore.

"Anything on two?" I ask Kincaid, in a reasonably calm voice.

He doesn't look at me, just buries his mouth in his microphone, breaking his transmission long enough to say, "No. Nothing."

"Right. . . . Okay. We're almost there. Keep with it."

I look out the side window, refocusing my thoughts. It was peaceful below. Farms sliding quietly beneath the nose and under the wings. A few fires burn off in the distance. "Controlled fires" denuding rich cane fields. Smoke rising vertically a few hundred feet before being whisked southwest by frictional winds. Havana is in a direct path. Many of the roadways look deserted and colored dusty red. But the countryside appears tranquil, even as it bakes itself raw in the broiling afternoon sun. I'm certain none of Fidel's people are aware of tension thundering in white contrails high overhead. We are almost in range of Miami Center when I hear the controller call our flight.

"Continental, 1866? If you read Miami, squawk code 1-3-2-7 and ident." It is welcome relief ending a dangerous situation. I twirl in the numbers and hit the 'ident' button in one quick motion, hoping Miami will receive our trace.

"Continental 1866 you are in radar contact," he replies, after a short delay. Cleared direct to Enamo intersection, flight plan route. Havana is aware of your radio problem and they wish you a safe flight. Switch to frequency 132.45."

What?... "Roger, Continental 1866," I speak into the microphone as though nothing has ever happened. My adrenal reserves depleted thirty long minutes ago. And for what? *Havana says, have a safe trip. That I shall, Señors. Did you wish the same to Brothers to the Rescue last year, before Raul's missiles slaughtered them?* I bid goodbye to phantasia land, then reprogram the computers and adjust the autopilot for a track 160 miles off-shore of Florida. Under my breath I thank the angels watching over me, asking them to: please convey my deepest respect to the Lord.

Three-and-one-half hours later, the radio altimeter wakes as we descend toward Newark's runway—22 Right—annunciating our height in feet above the touchdown zone. A male voice calling out: 100! 50! 30! 20! At 10, I raise the nose three degrees and slowly bring the throttles to idle. The eight main wheels slide onto concrete, spinning instantly to 148 knots. I relax the yoke, easing the nose tires to the rushing pavement, while at the same time pulling up on the reverse levers. The engine cowlings snap backwards forcing thrust forward, slowing us. We clear the runway, streamlining the wings, stowing the spoilers, and raising the flaps. The taxi to the ramp is relatively quiet.

At the gate, President Gutierrez comes forward, thanks me for a good flight, and autographs my logbook. I thank him too, for his confidence in me to join his political cabinet, but under the circumstances have to refuse his generous offer. He smiles in understanding, hesitates a moment, looking around the cockpit, then leaves.

I bow my head relieved to be home. *Almost home. Only an hour-and-a-half drive separating me from my family. Nothing compared with . . . with three nerve wracking days alone. I need an infusion. To calm the buzz still firing my nerves. To laugh with my wife and daughter. To enjoy my accomplishment. We made it. I made it.*

I leave some of the checklist duties to Kincaid. I want to say my farewells to the passengers as they deplane, and acknowledge—at least for me—a warm bond we formed and shared during the past five-and-a-half hours. They seem tired, yet happy, anxious to greet loved ones waiting in the gate area. The expectant mother comes forward. Her face glowing in a love I will never understand or be privileged to feel. I stand tall to meet the warmth of her aura. She holds one hand across her swelling abdomen and touches my hand with her other. "Gracias, Capi-tan," she says, looking deep into my eyes. I nod, turning with her as she steps into the jetway. "Bueñas Dias, Señora," I offer. She leaves a trail of love behind. The two lovers stride forward, giddy and animated. *I think they made it.* They smile at me, but don't stop. The plane empties quickly. Many shake my hand, others simply say, "goodbye." I'm at peace with myself having brought these people over 4,000 miles in safety. *Relative safety, Captain.* They should never know how tense it really was at times. People don't pay for that kind of knowledge. Only speed and comfort. Safety is a given, taken for granted like breathing. "That's it." I turn and make my way back to the flight deck.

I tell Kincaid he will have to repeat this qualification before he can fly back to South America. I don't add, "if ever," keeping that to myself. He looks at me with watery eyes. Not the eyes of confidence.

"People pay for our expertise," I add. "It's our job to meet that expectation . . . and more. We owe it to ourselves, too. Good luck. I'll advise training."

The drive home at rush hour, was like an experience in an IMAX theater. You can become part of the celluloid if you want, or with concerted effort, remain detached. I chose the latter and kept my dignity. Nothing seems relevant now. Not here, anchored by rubber to the ground. Not in this two-dimensional world. My mind drifts aimlessly, immune to the honking and cursing that blares all around me. It was war again. Just another ongoing battle over boundaries and closeness. I reach below the dash arming the ejection seat, turn up the music, and slide the 'Vette' into the slow lane. Rage and frustration are still around me. I see it etched deep in beautiful faces. But I didn't care. I saw it all too clearly hours ago—a world ago, back in Bogotá. *The price of intellect and reason. Our cost for being human.*

Ten miles ahead the traffic thins and I enjoy the view of northern Jersey's rolling hills and the sweet smell of pine trees and wild-flowers. Sanity loosens its grip on the harp strings stretched taut in my mind. I think my body is beginning to exude a tune all its own. I'm helpless against this soulful invitation, so I begin to sway with it. Then hum to it.

On March 17, 2001, Continental Flight 1866 took off from Quito, Ecuador, on what would be an eight-hour and eleven-minute flight. We started after a four-hour delay, flew into menacing fog and over the threatening Andes, risked being shot down over Cuba... and finally landed safely home—Newark Airport at 10:00 p.m.. Among the 185 passengers, the most famous, flying comfortably in first class, was Lucio Gutierrez, then El Presidente of Ecuador. Before he disembarked, President Gutierrez, who had earlier capriciously asked me to join his cabinet, stopped by the cockpit to autograph my logbook. A sweet reward for a long and hazardous flight.

REFLECTIONS

I didn't choose to fly, it chose me. I stepped into a maze, not aware that the entry gate was closing behind me, then it disappeared, leaving me stranded with a myriad of choices, but only one final outcome. I stumbled along pale corridors looking for reason and understanding. Each turn brought about an inkling of clarity, but nothing concrete, because I was too young in my journey. It was as though I had been handed a book of life, then asked to scour each page of mankind's existence, until I found what I was looking for. And what could that possibly be? What was I searching? Where do you hunt when you don't know what you're looking for? The path to *who am I, what am I*, bogs down in sediment as you claw trying to find yourself. Yet, it was there all along, in that blueprint set deep in the maze, and in a vision we call a dream. *A Dream.*

What is it that I saw? What sense was hidden there? What is its mystery? Are these visions merely questions churning in our minds, searching for answers? Do they exist because we are human, aware of our own existence? Do they swirl because we reason, then use logic against ourselves, and also against our planet? Everyone conjectures, but no one really knows.

Maybe dreams are . . . *purpose*, trying to speak to us? Maybe they are unfinished revelations, manifesting like broken thoughts? Ones that can be seen. We live through them in wonder. I lived through one . . . a very long time ago, and it still remains clear to me, even today:

Dancing Through The Maze

I'm there again, watching from a distance, looking down a very long road. Rolling hills, trees, and low brush line, each side. Everything seems to blend together. Nothing is distinct. A cambric curtain teasing my vision left and right, hinting at what lies beyond. Everything faraway, recedes into mist. Everything, except what is in front of me.

I move on it now. Rushing along. Racing faster and faster. I'm anchored to it. It is breathtaking, my heart races! Then suddenly it ends, and I'm whisked back to the beginning. And where I've been, I have no idea.

Night-after-night, I return to this same place, into this recurring journey. I have to live within it, each second of nighttime's minutes. Yet, there is comfort buried in that confusion.

I see my soul and spirit leaving for a time, visiting a place where my life should be. Maybe between the two, they see the future before I can live it, offering me back tomorrow as salvation.

Maybe they are night's messengers, returning at dawn, hoping I will discover understanding and recognize necessity, so they can be freed. So I can be free to follow a road that completes myself.

Maybe they are scripts of life, and I'm the actor reading.

Maybe they are filaments of my own self, floating in the background of my mind's eye, hoping I seize one final chance at life. One last attempt at choice. To exchange life in one maze, for fulfillment in another. Beyond that, all that remains is the play.

When they are satisfied, they return, disappearing in harmony within my body forever, setting me adrift—a cast away—dancing through the maze. Perhaps that's all it is.

So, I began to turn the pages, absorbing tendrils of life that slowly shaped a core into what was to become me. Elevating me into some recognizable form of self.

We are guests—protagonists—heroes, heroines, villains, and cowards written into our own biographies. A place where self and other can co-exist. Where undeniable truths force us toward recognition of something far greater than ourselves—the other. It begs belief in a Creator. Belief in a Spirit.

Every turn in the maze, each pathway down a corridor was a discovery of jewels. Precious stones existing for one purpose, to adorn my soul. Some of them brought happiness, others sorrow. But it was a journey I had to accept, because there was no other choice. Me alone, searching for enlightenment, which was not always easy. But neither was leaving behind gifted moments, or turning from people I had come to love so dearly. Every encounter brought richness that trailed like an eternal shadow. *A shadow.* That elegant stream of 'self,' illuminated forever by starlight.

Each page I turned brought history and wealth into my life. A more crafted vision of *who I am, what I am,* materializing like phosphoresence from mist. The momentum increased as I came to accept my place in *time* and in *space.* That physical arena we occupy here on Earth for such a brief time.

But there was always intrigue in the sky, for that shy, lonesome young man lost in the caverns of Brooklyn. Freedom beckoned up in the heavens. And the sun blazed yellow and red as I crisscrossed the maze. At times, I fell into the softness of billowing white clouds, and on occasion, had to endure the anger of black squalls. But they were necessary encounters in my development, bringing together knowledge, conviction, and strength. Perhaps not valor as one might imagine, but confidence and courage to face the capriciousness of life.

It was only a matter of time before I reached that final exit, where maturity releases you to freedom. Where I was freed at last, to mimic the gracefulness of raptors. I gained wings, soaring high with speeding winds, riding them in unison as we raced across the globe.

For thirty-five years I enjoyed that splendor. Brilliant discoveries uncovered as I meandered back and forth in the maze. Some of my friends asked, "What will you be when you grow up?" I had to smile because . . . because I saw what they apparently could not. That magical edge to life, so different from existing solely within it. Yet, no matter how I tried, I seemed to fail when I offered an explanation. If I told them "It's your *glory*, 'yourself and other' living in the moment, yet free," they would have turned away, scratching their heads, certain I was insane. But it is a consequence of all artists living in the moment, lost in their craft. And for whatever reason, my friends and I did not share sympathetic lives. We lacked resonance. And without alternative explanations, I had to walk away, too. I laughed a little bit, at myself, asking, "What *will you be* when you grow up, Bill?

Everything has an ending. When the circle fuses, the *end* is lost to the *beginning*. The math of life. The sine wave of the living as it finally pivots, metamorphosing into a circle. The cycle of life complete.

Twenty-four thousand hours aloft, and I was still a dreamer. Even when age and the government stepped in saying it was time to cease triviality and move along. Reluctantly, I did as they said, though not completely. I gave up larger machines for more agile smaller craft. I was greedy, still claiming ownership of the skies, flying for a few years after my retirement.

There is a phrase "Knowing When to Leave the Beach." It is borrowed. It was spoken to me by my close and longtime friend, Captain George Johnson. I thought it appropriate. I borrowed his phrase and constructed a diorama with words, flavoring each sentence with spices and delicacies, until there were no more. It is there in the Epilogue.

Flying has given me an eloquence of perception and a small trace of wisdom. The frailties of life become obvious. After all, once you strap into the cockpit of an airplane, light the engine and accelerate away from the earth, you are one with your machine. Self and other co-existing in paradox. You ride beside death because you want to live, to savor the preciousness this world offers. It adds sequins to your soul, so you sparkle even in darkness. It is with you always, freshness and wonder without life's jealousies. The Earth has no political boundaries when you look down from the sky. Only different geographical proportions.

Finally, I had to leave all this behind. George knew it. He had been there once himself. I thank him for his vision, for his logic and his friendship.

So, it happened one day, without premeditation, that I simply set the brakes of my plane, gathered my charts and belongings, climbed down from the cockpit and folded my wings . . . forever.

I still navigate the maze, but with a more genteel respect and wisdom for its grace. *Don't we all?*

Dancing Through The Maze

EPILOGUE

I took the ceremony to Bass Harbor, Maine, where treachery finds love with elegance. A five square mile coastal island of quiet and a sanctuary for personal reflection.

A place where tormented African winds sweep west across the vast Atlantic, gathering freshness, releasing its flavor here and over the Cranberry Islands. A place where ocean rollers broil like spurned lovers racing in magnified fury toward Harbor Head Lighthouse, crashing with choir deepness against the rock cliffs.

There is an out-cropping I remember below the harbor master's cottage, where spray from the waves falls like scattered seeds, bringing renewed vigor to your face and life to your soul. A place where the currents are too strong and the waters too dangerous to explore. A proper place for . . . for the end of my beginning.

My body ached from the weight of the backpack; thirty pounds of uniforms, four ounces of Vietnam Campaign and Air medals, and fifty pounds of culpability to weigh it all down. Decorations of a ghost. I wanted to add more resentment, but at my age, the additional weight prevented me. It was war that I hated, not the sky. Just a continuing paradox, hate and love vying for equal space. *Freedom billows in the shadow of strength. Invasion necessitates argument for the consequences of that might. And it is the innocent who suffer most, who ask only . . . Let us be. How unfortunate, abuse written in blood throughout the history of mankind. When will it end? Where is reason? Will we ever learn decency?* I inhaled deeply while closing my eyes, shaking my head in disbelief at our own travesties, then I leaned into the wind and spray, balanced myself carefully over the rocks, and let the pack drop into the ocean.

In time the sea and wild currents will rip away the bindings. The fabric will rot and the medals oxidize. But the disgust . . . will drift forever. Diluted, yes. But always running.

I was about to toss my gold airline wings too, but stopped. *How could I? Why? Flying was my love. Her wings my comfort. She was my lover-my friend, my escape from a sane society. And she deserved better.* Yet, I had to let her go, too. With dignity. So I kept the wings, but freed her memories.

There was no loud report when the heavy sack struck the water, sinking rapidly beneath the waves. The rushing wind past my ears and the pounding surf obscured it. I stared down, almost in disbelief, as a part of my life turned emerald, then disappeared. The ever-gnawing questions: When is enough . . . enough? When is it time? When do you walk away? They were finally answered. There could be no return. I was no Phoenix. Age and maturity have seen to that.

"You have to know when to leave the beach. Yes," I said to myself, then turned my back to the sea. For me, *when. . .was* now.

A blazing afternoon sun lifted the spray from my face. The warmth was hypnotic and I stayed transfixed for many moments.

Finally, I looked up, contemplating the rugged cliff in front of me, slowly climbing over the wet rocks. . .Making my own path away from the beach. Then disappeared into the maze, searching for . . .What is to be.